God Must Be A Man!

God Must Be A Man!

What Women Have To Go Through That Men Don't

Elizabeth Caproni

Think Big Press
www.thinkbigpress.com

Published in the United Kingdom by:

Think Big Press
www.thinkbigpress.com

© Elizabeth Caproni, 2008

A catalogue for this book is available from the British Library.

ISBN 978-0-9558599-0-8

Printed and bound by CPI Antony Rowe, Eastbourne

For my Mum...who bore the pain of childbirth to bring me into this world!

Contents

Acknowledgements

I would firstly like to thank my wonderful and amazing partner, Dr. David Hamilton, who makes my life magical. His perpetual love, and unrelenting support and belief in me, has enabled this book to happen. (Note to David: Chapter Four doesn't apply to you!!)

I would also like to thank my wonderful and amazing parents, Elma and Peter Caproni, who have always encouraged me to follow my heart and my dreams. Without their support, I would not be where I am today. I hope that when I have children, I will be as much of an inspiration to them, as my Mum and Dad have been to me.

A big thank-you also, to all who contributed to this book. I am so grateful to all the ladies who gave me their stories, and especially those who were brave enough to let me include their names in the book! To those who asked to remain anonymous: your secret is safe with me!

And last, but certainly not least, thank you to God for taking this book in the way it is meant to be perceived - a bit of fun! You know I love ya really!

Introduction

I have found myself, on numerous occasions, shouting out, 'God Must Be A Man!' This usually happens when I am experiencing some form of discomfort that only ladies experience e.g. period pains, aching feet from a pair of killer heels, or a sore and bloated belly from holding in some, ahem, gas, as society (men) dictates, 'Ladies aren't supposed to let their wind break free.' (I will explain in the book how God created this unfairness!)

And so the more I found myself complaining about the pain of womanhood, the more I realised that men don't have half the amount to grumble about, compared to women. Things just aren't balanced out at all. Women have so much more palaver: menstruating, invasive examinations, biological clocks ticking away, and the mother of all pain: giving birth!

In stark contrast, the first unpleasant process a guy goes through is having a prostate check in his FIFTIES!! It's hardly fair!

So this got me thinking that we must indeed have a male creator, like a typical "lad" looking out for his mates. I mean, think about it. If we had a female maker, then I think that the physical pain would be shared out a little more equally between the two sexes, don't you?

So I feel it my duty to expose this sham that God loves all of humanity equally. He clearly has his male buddies interests at heart first and foremost. And so I reveal how, by programming humankind with certain "chips", he made life easier for the guys.

So, in my opinion, after thousands of years and billions of women suffering, it's high time God rectified his "mistakes".

In this book, after pointing out the colossal amount of unfair absurdities that women have to endure, I ask God to tone things down a little - so the next batch of females who come to earth can be a bit more pain and hassle free!

Enjoy!

Chapter One

Not A Girl...Not Yet A Woman

A lot of people may already believe that God is a man. They imagine him to be a big bearded man up in the sky on a cloud, staring sternly down upon us and judging our every move. Other people, however, believe that God is a woman. They want to believe in a more feminine and gentle energy, and to be honest, are probably quite sick of men and their dominance. And then there are others who believe that God is neither a man nor a woman. To them, God is energy of some sort, existing in every dimension.

Now I could probably get on board with the latter. I am, after all, quite a spiritual person and want to believe that we are being looked after in a non-discriminatory way, with God understanding and creating both sexes with equal opportunities in mind.

However, my life journey so far has led me to believe that this isn't quite the case. I believe that God is in fact a man - not like the stern bearded one, more like one of the lads - and not the best of designers. I can't help but feel that he looked out for the guys a "tad" more when he was designing humanity. I reckon when he was deciding on the differences between the male and the female anatomy, he just lumped all the painful nonsense with the ladies, earning him an almighty and testosterone filled cheer from his male assistants (mates) in heaven.

Now please don't get the impression that I am too much of a raving mad feminist, because I'm not. I mean, I'm all for equal opportunities etc., but I still love to have a man open a door for me and let me go first, and for him to pull my chair out for me to sit down to dinner. I find that really attractive and charming. It's just that God went too far. He didn't balance things out. He made guys want to act tougher than women, but gave women all the physical pain to suffer - that doesn't make sense and is *soooooooo* unfair.

I believe that God has placed lots of different genes inside women so that their lives will be harder and men's, by comparison, will be easier. Basically, he let his mates off the hook. For example, I think he placed "Serve Your Man" genes inside women when humanity began. Over time, however, this gene has perhaps "weakened" since women's lib erupted, causing women to be a lot stronger and more vocal about their rights to work etc., and so they won't "serve" their man quite as much.

You see, my partner, Dr. David Hamilton, is a scientist and author of the books, "It's The Thought That Counts", "Destiny Versus Free Will" and the forthcoming "How The Mind Can Heal The Body" (yes, I thought I'd give him a little plug!), and I have recently discovered that we can affect our DNA - we aren't stuck with what we are given! Apparently our genes can express in different ways through our thoughts and emotions, and so I think that's why some genes (I actually prefer to call them "chips" as I feel we have been programmed like the Stepford Wives) placed in women since the beginning of humanity, have become "less efficient" due to "Girl Power".

So the more determined and stronger us women get, those "chips" might have a tougher time controlling us! N.B. I will point out the chips to be aware of throughout the book.

But God gave us other genes/chips that are more difficult to control than others. Yes, God also gave us ones that make women's bodies do embarrassing things e.g. how our bodies create more gas when pregnant. I mean, there is really no need for this to happen, and so I can only assume that this is down to God's wicked sense of humour.

Yes, I think God created those kind of "chips" to bring him some comic relief when down in the dumps with having to answer so many prayers for tragedies around the world.

I mean, it seems obvious to me that God is a male — everything up until this point is referred to as HIStory. Yes, HIS STORY! I'm sure if God was a female, it would be referred to as HERstory. Yes, whilst God was penning HIS STORY down, I'm sure he must have been racking his brain on trying to decide on what women should endure, so as to make his male "soul mates" lives easier for when they incarnate on earth.

So, I believe that in this book, I have collated enough evidence to prove that women have definitely not had a fair deal in the creation of humanity and I am sure you will agree with me after reading it, especially if you are of the female species.

Growing Pains!

I felt very grown up when my Mum took me shopping for my first bra. A 28 AA, if I recall correctly, was the size of my very first one. Before then I was wearing a little camisole top to "support" my, ahem, "breasts", if you could call them that.

This was the beginning of womanhood. I started noticing scary words and terms in my Mother's magazines that I shouldn't have been reading - Polycystic Ovaries, Fibroids, Endometriosis, Hot Flushes, Thrush, Bleeding, Hysterectomy, PMT, BML, HRT, a VPL… 'What *are* all of these?!' I remember thinking, with my eyes popping out of my head. The only abbreviation that I knew of was a BLT from Burger King.

Not liking the sound of the words in the magazine, I shut them out of my head. I had enough to deal with at that time. I was 11 years old and developing breasts, which was not only embarrassing but really painful as well. Boys in my class would stare at the two tiny little things on my chest that had just begun to sprout, not realising the agony of growing pains that I was suffering with it. I remember thinking that this can't be right, there must be something wrong with me, why was I in so much pain? I especially thought that there was something wrong, and felt more freakish than ever, when one breast started to grow faster than the other!

'What the hell?'

A Pad To Cushion The Blow

I turned twelve, and at this point in my life - an innocent young lady - I had no inclination that God was a typical bloke and fell short of being a fully qualified designer. I mean, I was a little bit in pain, but it was worth it if I was going to get breasts! I could cope with that. Ah, how sweet and naïve, I had no idea how corrupt it was about to get.

Out of nowhere sprung hideous stomach pains, ugly mood swings, hair sprouting out of every orifice, and after a few months - aghhhh! - my period arrives. Wow! 'MUM!' I remember shouting, panic stricken but with a touch of excitement. 'Look,' I said. My Mum, shocked and a tad emotional, hugged me, giving me the proud look of, 'There's my little girl becoming a woman,' and went to get me what she called a "little towel".

Waiting in anticipation for my "discreet" little friend to arrive, I sat there, feeling grown-up.......tender, but mature. It dawned on me that this was the "bleeding" they were talking about in my Mum's magazine – I had started my periods! This made me feel great. I wasn't a little girl anymore! I was a woman! (Although, I wasn't too keen on any of the other stuff that I read about, so I was hoping that this was my lot......again, how wonderfully naïve).

My Mother arrived back and, as if in slow motion, revealed a mammoth sized pad almost the size of a pillow. I was speechless. My excitement of being a woman lessened considerably and expeditiously. But after a few moments taking in the enormity of this elephant sized sanitary wear, I regained some composure and followed my Mother's instructions on how to wear it, like a soldier to their Commanding Officer.

After a few moments of just trying to fit the bloody thing (no pun intended!) onto my pants, I then had the task of trying to walk with it. Now bearing in mind that I had a pair of leggings clinging to my skinny little legs and bottom, I waddled from the hallway into the kitchen and back with my Mum watching as if I were modelling the latest fashions on the catwalk in Milan. The "only" difference was that I felt and looked like Donald Duck. I felt like I was wearing a nappy! How could I live the rest of my life like this??? Would I be able to ever run, swim, sit, just even walk like a normal person ever again?

Need To Down Size!

This felt very wrong. I wore those ridiculously over-sized pads for about a week desperately looking for an alternative protector. I searched and searched, until eventually a lovely little thin towel with angelic wings came floating into my life which, by comparison, was the size of an alarm clock to the almighty Big Ben I had been wearing. Sheer bliss! Well, ok, not quite. It was still an intrusion into my life to wear any such thing in my underwear, and one week a month of pain, bleeding and sacrificing my swimming time was highly annoying. 'God,' I thought, sitting on the side of my local swimming pool watching boys splashing about, 'Why don't boys have any of this?' I guess that was my first unconscious thought that God must be one of the guys.

After converting my Mum to the alarm clock from Big Ben, (which she thought was a miracle and couldn't believe the difference) I was on a roll. After reading some more magazines that were far too advanced for my years, I took her to the shops to get me (and her) an under-wired bra. Yes, my first bra and my Mother's bra's were wireless and, well to put it mildly, rubbish. If my breasts were going to be on show to the world underneath my tops, then I was damn sure they were going to look good! My Mum, again, was converted and wondered where her little girl was getting all this advice.

I felt like I was coping quite well with the transition from a girl to a woman, considering it was quite painful. I was a novice in womanhood and *I* was teaching my Mother stuff, I was taking to this like a duck to water…or so I thought.

An Unexpected Visitor

Having the monthly visitor that I was now getting used to, I realised that just before my due date, I had to be prepared and armed with some sort of protection everywhere I went. It was all going so well until I was caught out for the first time…in a shopping mall.

Yes, I was taken by surprise by an early visit due to excitement and anticipation about seeing my beloved Take That in concert. I went to the toilet confused by the pains I was having, and couldn't believe it! My period had arrived a whole *week* early! This was uncalled for! This was not on! This was…very new. 'I thought this was just supposed to happen once a month at almost the exact same time,' I thought (ah yes, there's that naive thing again). So as I was caught out so early, I didn't have any protection with me. 'Oh – my – God,' I thought, 'What the hell do I do?'

My Mum was in another shop and this was in the day when not every man, woman, child and pet had a mobile phone, so there was no way of putting out an SOS call. With the queue outside this single cubicle toilet growing and the patience of it getting less and less and my face getting more and more like a beetroot, there was only one thing I could do: I folded lots and lots of toilet paper and stuffed it into my knickers, with the task in mind that I would just buy a little towel from the machine next to the sinks and then go back into the toilet to put one on, and everything would be ok. 'Phew, yes, there's my plan,' I thought.

Acting nonchalant, I flushed the loo and opened the door to an almighty queue and headed towards the sinks. I washed my little shaking hands and took out my purse to purchase a towel from the machine…only to find that there were no towels on sale - only tampons. Yikes! I had never tried *them* before! I had heard stories that if you put them up too far they would get lost - and you could die! I panicked. I quickly wondered what my options were. Number 1: I just leave and pray that the toilet paper will do the job until I find my Mum to rescue me. Number 2: I could purchase a tampon and try to figure out what the hell to do with it. Or number 3: Collapse on the floor and flake out and start crying for my Mum like a big cry-baby.

Now, as much as number 3 was very appealing, I thought that I should try to be a little bit more grown up, seeing as I was experiencing women's problems. So I decided on number 1. But just as I started to walk out of the loo, I felt the toilet paper travel south to my ankle and I came to a startled halt. Oh my God, it was going to have to be number 2. So I bought a box of tampons, not quite sure if I was choosing the right absorbency: mini lite, lite, regular, super, super plus…the list was endless! I chose the super ones, hoping that they were going to be as wonderful as they sounded - staying away from the super plus, as they just sounded too good to be true.

I eventually got back into the cubicle, when it had thankfully quietened down a bit. I read the instructions and tried to insert the tampon…only there was one problem - I had no idea where it was supposed to go!

Staring at the illustration of a lady on the instructions, I shakily balanced on one leg whilst lifting my other, as this was, apparently, supposed to make it easier to insert (!!??). I fiddled about, praying to find the entrance sometime soon, as if in a maze and desperately trying to find my way out - only I was trying to find my way in. I eventually just gave up, worried that I was going to die if I did it the wrong way. I collapsed on the loo in a mixed state of fear and surrender. I had no clue what to do next. I had had enough. Being a woman was just too tough.

Thankfully my Mother eventually came into the toilet and rescued me from my tricky situation. But I wasn't going to be caught out again. From that day onwards, I decided to be prepared at all times; like a soldier in battle, and I definitely wasn't going to go near a tampon for a good while yet.

Hair Hair Everywhere

Next came hair. Not the kind on your head, although that was looking a little awful with all the hairspray I was caking it with. No, this hair was everywhere. I couldn't pretend that nobody noticed it anymore. It was in fact, time for my first shave. Not like a boy's first shave that is just his face! Oh no! For us girls it's a head to toe job, well, an underarm to toe job.

I remember my Mum handing me a strange little shell shaped razor and telling me that at 12 years old I was too young to be shaving my legs and that, once I started, that would be me for the REST OF MY LIFE. Now, as scary a thought as that was, I took the razor and sunk into the hot bath. A last comment from my Mum came through the bolted door, 'Be careful, TRY NOT TO CUT YOURSELF.'

My heart was pounding. Thoughts and images were racing through my head of blood pouring from my legs and having to be rushed to accident and emergency. The steam from the bath condensing only added to the sweat already dripping from my brow. I started having second thoughts: 'Maybe I am too young. Maybe you can't see the hairs on my legs.'

Just as I was about to chicken out and leave what was now becoming a tepid bath, I looked down on my legs one last time and thought, 'Who am I kidding, you can see them from a mile off.'

So I took a deep breath and very carefully manoeuvred the razor up my lower leg and removed the first patch of hair. I was overjoyed! It didn't hurt, and as far as I could see there was no need for a 999 call! I continued to remove the rest of my hair jubilantly with just a few nicks here and there. I basked in my triumph. I had hair-free legs! Woo-hoo! They felt so smooth! I wore a pair of shorts that day to show them off and glanced at them in the mirror at every opportunity I got.

It wasn't until the next morning when I woke up and the smoothness had turned to stubble, that I felt quite disillusioned. 'You mean I have to go through all that *again*?!' Life as a woman wasn't quite cracking up to what I thought it would be.

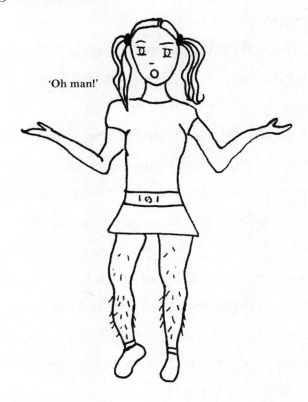

'Oh man!'

God Ain't Versace

To me, a great designer is one who produces something that looks fabulous, is preferably comfortable, and can be looked after without a great deal of maintenance. Now do you call body hair, along with the pain and hassle of removing it, a good design? No, I thought not. This is what I am talking about. God is obviously a typical man, as no woman would have such flaws in her design. Ok, granted, there are a lot of fabulous male designers in the world, but they tend to be, well, quite feminine.

God has had good cover up 'til now. You see, I was brought up Catholic and regularly went to church as a child. During those years, I was taught how wonderful God was; that God created the earth and all of humanity, helps those that are suffering, and is generally there for everyone. Now, whilst I greatly admire all of God's humanitarian efforts and I am grateful for being helped out in times of need in the past, I think that what the church teachings left out was, when it came to women, God blatantly decided to take the piss (probably whilst having a drink with the lads), and so women have come off the worst.

But don't get me wrong. Women are beautiful and strong. What I am talking about here is the intricate design. I think that there are some major flaws in the interior and exterior that should have been more carefully sketched out before (drunkenly) hopping onto the sewing machine and taking orders.

I mean lets think about it. If you were to design a being that was supposed to be feminine, sexy and alluring, would you give them hair under their arms, around their bikini line and on their legs? (Not to mention that some women even have moustaches and beards...now that's just taking the **major** piss if you ask me)

No, I thought not. Women like to look good and know what looks good. No woman in her right mind would choose to put hair on all of womankind. Hair on women looks terrible, is time consuming and ridiculously painful to remove (Waxing...ouch! My Mum had her legs waxed in preparation for going on holiday once. She nearly fainted at the pain and her legs looked like they had caught the measles - she has stuck to shaving ever since). An obvious indication that God is male, I think.

And why would you design a woman to have inconvenient periods every month? Couldn't it have been done in a different way? Like, as in, no periods at all?

Then sex. Yes, it is a lot more complex for women. Not quite so "simple" and as "straightforward" as it is for men, if you know what I mean.

Then there is pregnancy. Women's lives are affected enormously; their jobs put on hold because they have to carry and nurse the child, whereas the man can just carry on as normal.

Then there's the "wonder" of childbirth - a major, *major* flaw if you ask me. Now at this point in my life, I am not yet a Mother, but from what I have heard, trying to squeeze a watermelon through a hole the size of a lemon is not quite what I would have had in mind for a fun time.

Cellulite - more like celluheavy! If the cells were "lite" then we wouldn't have this problem, would we? Yes, *another* wonderful curse on the female species! No matter how hard we work out and eat a low fat diet, it still raises its ugly head. Men? They don't have this problem - women have more fat cells.

Becoming increasingly suspicious isn't it? I think you must be beginning to see that we indeed have an under par male designer and females are definitely bearing the brunt of it.

I will touch more on some of those subjects above later in the book. One subject missing from that list however, is the incredibly appealing and much looked forward to invasive vaginal examinations. I'm sorry, it had to be touched upon. Approach next chapter with caution.

Chapter Two

Time For Inspection

So by this time, a few years on, women have now become rather accustomed to period pains, hair removal and managing to control their PMT by getting their hands on a punch bag and a voodoo doll. But hold on! This physical and emotional rollercoaster ride is about to get a lot more intense…and intimate.

Yes, I'm talking about the

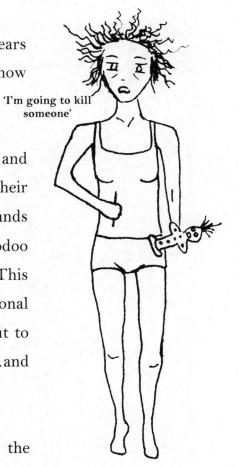

'I'm going to kill someone'

wonderful invasive vaginal examinations! As if we haven't had enough to contend with, but we now have to go and have our nether region inspected as well.

Exam Time

'What the hell are those dimples on my legs?'

Yes, when a young woman is coming to her late teens/early twenties, coping with being a woman gets that little bit tougher. For instance, most are introduced to their new little "dimple friends for life" on their thighs and bum. Up until then, you probably had a tight little ass and perfect pins, and the thought, 'My God, these are far too short!' never so much as entered your head. The need to dismiss hot pants and the micro mini only adds to your waning life as a carefree girl.

Then, you receive a mysterious letter through the post. To your horror, you find that you are due for your first invasive vaginal examination! Yes, for all women, this is the step-up in the "inspection"… this is the beginning of a lifetime of invasive vaginal examinations!

This is yet another obstacle that men don't have (ok, except the prostate check that men have in their fifties, which, granted, is not at all pleasant, but c'mon guys, you practically have a lifetime to prepare for that one. In my opinion, that certainly does not balance out being stared, poked and prodded at from the tender age of 19/ 20!)

For my first examination, I made absolutely sure that I was having a female inspector and not a male one. Some women don't have a problem with having a male doctor inspecting "downstairs" but I just can't imagine lying half naked and have a male fiddle about down there, without being horribly mortified when bumping into him at the supermarket in the cereal aisle. I mean, how would that conversation go? 'How are you?' the doctor would say. 'Oh, yep, my vagina is doing just great thanks…thanks for checking it out the other day, by the way.' And then if a friend appeared on the scene asking who my gentleman friend was, what would I say? 'Oh, he just looks at my vagina from time to time,' with the friend moving curiously and quickly onto the next aisle.

A Cheeky Moment

A girl I know of had quite an experience whilst having an examination "down there". Her usual (female) doctor was away and the only doctor that was available to see her that day was a friend of her family – and male. She was mortified. However, she didn't want to offend him by asking for another doctor for this particular problem she had, so plucked up the courage and thought, 'I'm sure it will be just fine. It will be over and done with sooner than I think and I shouldn't be embarrassed because that is just silly, I'm a grown woman and he is a professional.'

So there she was, at the surgery, managing to remain dignified and reserved whilst removing her knickers. As she lay down and stared at the ceiling, she started humming to herself in her mind, pretending that she was used to this kind of invasion, whilst the friend of the family Doctor "attended" to her. 'La la la, hum de dum. This is perfectly natural,' she thought, 'I don't know why I was so worried about him giving my vagina the onceover.'

Then, to her horror and almost as if the universe timed it to perfection, her phone went off in her bag that was lying on the floor next to her, blaring out the ring-tone: 'THE CHEEKY SONG (TOUCH MY BUM)' from the Cheeky Girls! Yes, the lyrics, 'COME AND SMILE DON'T BE SHY, TOUCH MY BUM THIS IS LIFE' just kept rolling on out and made the examination feel like they were doing stuff that they shouldn't. '*Pleeeease,*' she silently and desperately prayed, with her face pulsating with the incredible amount of blood that had rushed there, 'Hurry up and just go to voicemail!' After a few more of the ingenious lyrics, it finally did. Paralyzed with utter humiliation, she could barely move to get her knickers back on.

Since that day, she has always made sure that her phone is switched off whenever she visits the doctor's surgery.

Something similar happened to another girl I know. The male doctor was asking about her holiday in Arizona. Then, just as the doctor parted her legs, he said, 'THE GRAND CANYON IS AMAZING ISN'T IT?'

Well, I guess those examinations are quite important to have done to make sure that there is nothing wrong, but it's so unfair considering men have squat to go through!

What The Hell Is That?!

But what is perhaps more disturbing, is the fact that whilst women are going to have their vagina checked out by another human being, most have probably never checked their vagina out themselves! I mean, I think that there are a lot of women that don't have a clue what their vagina even looks like. But this is through no fault of their own because, lets be honest, we can barely see the bloody thing!

'What the hell was that???'

32

Men have no problem in this area, their apparatus is quite apparent, plus the fact that they constantly fiddle about with themselves, means they are more than familiar with what everything looks *and* feels like.

But for a woman? Well, it's a little more difficult to see what the hell we have down there. This was demonstrated perfectly in an episode of Sex And The City when Charlotte admits that she has never seen herself "down there", and so later she cautiously takes a mirror and places it beneath her, only to keel over at the sight that was presented to her.

But isn't this ridiculous? We have all this palaver of squatting over mirrors and trying to identify all the different parts - where things come out of, where things should go in, what bit is supposed to give us pleasure...we practically have to do a course in human biology just to figure out just what and where the hell everything is! I *still* don't know where everything is! I don't think there's a woman alive who does! Apart, obviously, from female doctors – but isn't that saying something!

We even have to make sure that our vagina isn't in a bad mood! An imbalanced pH level can lead to Thrush, causing a very upset vagina!

Whereas with a guy, they pretty much have everything laid out for them in a simple and easy to use format with no need to worry if they are upsetting their genitals, or indeed, if their nether region is emitting signals that dogs can pick up on.

Not To Be Sniffed At!

Quite a few years ago, I experienced - several times - my neighbour's dog, Bosun, a beautiful golden Labrador, sniffing, ahem, "downstairs" when I was menstruating. I mean, how humiliating is that for a female?! Trying to have a polite conversation with your neighbour, whilst at the same time trying to manoeuvre their dog's face from your vagina is quite mortifying. I mean, it's now pretty obvious to everyone what time of the month it is.

What also shouts out loud and clear to the world that you're on your period is when you have to buy some "feminine care". This may just be me, but I still get embarrassed at picking up a box of tampons, especially if it is the *only* thing you are buying, then putting them into the transparent shopping basket (there is just no disguising them!) and then realising that the only available till-point has a male assistant serving. The heart sinks – you have to put this brightly coloured box on a *huge* conveyer belt, with time then deciding to just tick by at a leisurely pace, matching the slow and corny music playing in the supermarket.

Then, only to add to the crushing experience, a male customer appears behind you, waiting to see when the lonely box of tampons will reach the assistant's till, so that he can start loading his shopping onto the belt. And then the spotty teenage assistant stares at you as he "beeps" the tampons through.

Yes, there's not another experience like it to proclaim to the world, 'Yes, that's right, I'm on my period, glad you noticed!'

It's A Jungle Out There

And at this stage in life, it's not just your nether region that begins to be inspected thoroughly. For instance, going out with my girlfriends when I was at this age (19/20), was always an experience. A group of 3 young women just looking forward to getting together for a chit-chat and a laugh over a cocktail or two was always accompanied by the kind observations of young gentlemen on a street corner that we had to walk past to get to our destination.

Our hearts always began beating faster as we got nearer them, trying to look away, praying that we could just get past them without being seized upon; as if we were the wildebeest on the plains of Africa trying to cross the river and not get eaten by one of the angry crocs. But, just like the wildebeest, who were we kidding?

'Cor, look at the size of her tits,' was always one observation. Another was, 'I prefer the one with the small pointy ones,' to the incredibly complimentary, 'That one is as flat as a pancake,' ending on one of my most beloved songs, 'Take your top off for the lads.' It was always so romantic to be serenaded in public with such poetic words…who needed Shakespeare?

After quite a few of those Serengeti moments, it started to make sense to me as to why so many women in society are so obsessed about the size of their breasts. And why there are so many young girls having surgery to enhance them…or to reduce them if they are overly big - girls tend to know if this is the case if men don't even notice they have a face. (Note to men: we can tell where you are looking).

This, I feel is another unfair advantage in the design of the two sexes. Woman can't tell from a man, in just seeing him in a pair of trousers or jeans, what the size of his penis is. Can you imagine if we could? Oh boy! Can you imagine the sheer panic in them? Not only would there be padded bras for women, but padded pants for men, in an array of sizes.

And I'm sure that the request for penis extension surgery would greatly outnumber the current figure for breast enhancements. The tables would be turned. Men would walk down the street and women would comment, 'Pah, look at the size of that, how pathetic,' and laugh. With their red faces and a taste of their own medicine, I'm sure that there would be no longer any comments on ladies breasts and the typical self assured "Romeo" would no longer be quite so cocky (No pun intended!).

However, unfortunately, this is not reality, and it's the young women who are being scrutinised. I mean, all that women at this stage in life have to put up with compared to men is hardly fair.

Whilst I and my female companions were trying to identify all the components of our vagina, figuring out an alternative route to the cocktail bar so to avoid hearing lyrics about our breasts, and deciding on what doctor to reveal all to, all that the young men of the same age had to think about was what computer game they were going to play that night, what club they were going to party at the weekend and hoping to pull a hot chick when they got there.

Yes, the female journey is a tough and painful one, which brings me onto my next subject - fashion.

Chapter Three

Fashionistas

When it comes to clothes, women love to shop, granted. I love to look my best no matter what it takes. But at the end of one, long, rather unsuccessful day's shopping when my feet felt they were going to fall off, I started to think that men had the better deal here - and perhaps have always had the better deal.

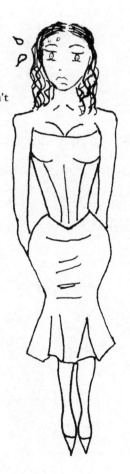

'Help, I can't breathe!'

Ladies in Victorian times went through sheer hell for the fashionable corseted look. Their internal organs were squished closer together and out of their original positions, along with their lung volume diminishing, which lead to inter-costal breathing. And apparently some ladies even got down to a twelve-inch waist! Yikes!

Today's fashion is perhaps not quite as painful (although we do have stilettos!) but it can still take an awful lot of rigmarole.

Preparation Is Everything

Ok, we may not have to have an assistant to compress us into a boned corset nowadays, but when it comes to getting ready for a night out, this is when the unfairness really becomes apparent between the sexes.

For women, after deciding on what shape we are – pear, apple, or hourglass – and feeling like a donkey after realising we also have saddlebags – we can then start to choose the right style of outfit to wear for a big night out…but it can take a while.

Most of us really start getting ready weeks in advance - fake tanning ourselves and picking out potential nail colours. However, on the actual night, what we sometimes envisage to look good on us, can in reality not quite be the case, and so it's a major panic to find something – *anything!* - to wear.

It's a case of, 'Should I wear a dress, jeans, trousers or a skirt?' And if we decide on the skirt, it's then a case of, 'Should I wear the circulation restrictive tights, the slippery stockings or brave it and just go bare legged?'

Then once we have decided on the outfit we are going to wear, we then have to decide on the underwear that is required to go with it - 'Am I going to have a VPL? Do I need to wear the thong (*please no!*) or should it be the seamless pants?' (Thank heavens for the creation of Spanx pants!) Then, 'What bra do I wear - the strapless or the one with the transparent straps? Or should I go for the little cups that stick to my breasts?'

Then it's the feet. The kitten heels or stilettos? An open or a closed toe? Platforms boots or the just the regular ones? And that's just the style. That's not even deciding on the colour!

Then there's the hair: straight or curly? Up or down? And the make-up and nails: dramatic or natural?

We then have to accessorise - the big dangly earrings or the small studs? The bangles or just the watch? The big glitzy ring or the smaller, subtler one? Then there's the choice of bag - which colour and style goes best? The small black clutch or the silver over the shoulder?

These are only *some* of the questions that pop up on a women's preparation for a night out…and men wonder why we take so long to get ready!!!

For a man? Well, they shower, slip on their boxers, jump into their jeans, throw on the shirt, fiddle about with their hair for a few seconds, slap on a bit of cologne… and that's them. Then they sit with a beer whilst they wait on us getting ready. Sickening isn't it?

Wardrobe Malfunction

Yes, deciding what look to go for can take women a while. And after all the effort we go to, a woman's worst nightmare is — yes, you've guessed it - turning up to an event with the same dress on as another lady.

Mortifying! We've literally spent weeks on getting ready, and then all you wanna do is get the hell out of there at lightning speed!

Again, men do not have this problem. They all practically look the same anyway – tuxes and suits - they never have the dreaded thought of, 'I hope no one else is wearing this,' because they are expected to all dress similarly.

'Mm, it feels a bit draughty'

There is also another look that definitely does not wear well with women, and all women everywhere must take assertive action if they ever see a woman with this look in public and tell them about their excruciatingly terrible fashion error - it's the SKIRT TUCKED INTO YOUR PANTS LOOK.

A few years ago, my friend was on a shopping spree and after a nice little cup of tea and a scone - which is a required element in a day's shopping for her - she went to the toilet before continuing with her day of purchasing.

A short while after, my friend, whilst browsing the Home Interior Department in the store, felt like it was a little draughty, but put that down to the air conditioning. It wasn't until a little lady with an admirable amount of compassion (compared to the other sniggering spectators that just let the undignified show continue) came up to her and told her that her bottom was on show, that my friend knew she had committed this fashion faux pas.

When things like that happen, it's hard to try and maintain your dignity. However, there are many more fashion related incidents that can happen that also make you wish the ground would open up and swallow you. I have personally named them all:

THE TWIST – going over your ankle and nearly falling flat on your face whilst trying to act cool in killer heels, just as you are passing a group of people – mortifying!

THE CINDERELLA - when the heel of your shoe gets stuck in the grooves on a pavement in town, and you accidentally walk on without the shoe.

THE CELEB - when your strap from your dress falls down and reveals more than you wish for all to see.

THE MARILYN MONROE - wind blowing your skirt up in your face just as a whole load of traffic comes by.

This one happened to me when I was entering a church wedding. A gust of wind blew my skirt up, revealing my **flesh** coloured knickers (some people thought I wasn't wearing any!) and taking my fascinator from my head also. And it was all caught on video. Lovely.

Here Comes The......Disaster!

Again, this is another unfair design flaw. Men don't wear skirts and so don't have to worry about doing an involuntary moony...well, I suppose they maybe do sometimes, if they are Scottish and at a wedding.

Yes, I have been to quite a few weddings in Scotland where the wind can definitely blow high, and it is quite a scary moment when the groom reveals he is a "true Scotsman" when his kilt blows over his head.

Again, this is another thing that is better for men; women have a much more "concealed" anatomy "down there" to look at and most men quite enjoy having a glance. However, most women I know think that a guy is much sexier with his boxers on than off. So for us girls, it's definitely a, 'Donald where's your troosers?' situation…as in, find them and keep them on!

Yes, weddings are much more of a hassle for women than men. It's all about looking perfect, and corseted underwear that you can't breathe in.

I was bridesmaid at my cousin's wedding and it was a fight to see who would catch the bouquet of flowers between myself and the other bridesmaid. We were both trying to act nonchalant, even though we were actually like two sprinters in their blocks, nervously waiting for the bang from the gun. As soon as Susan (my cousin) threw her bouquet in the air, we were off, and both launched forward like a couple of American football players going in for a tackle, but as Marian (the other bridesmaid) grabbed the bouquet, her restrictive dress burst open and all her buttons popped off the back! So it was an emergency sewing job right away - and all this was going on whilst the men were ordering themselves a pint! So unfair!

A Sticky Situation

Yes, the clothes for women are so much more complicated - big buttons, ribbons, clips and fidgety zips at the back and side. It can take an age to just get the damn clothes on! And don't even get me started on trying to figure out how to put on a criss-cross strap dress!

Even bags can be tricky. My good friend Olivia had one of those fashionably over-sized *monster* bags with her when she took her teenage daughter and her friends to Magic Mountain theme park in LA. It was one of those days when she was particularly pre-menopausal, cranky, spacey, irritated. Basically "out to lunch". Her having to listen to blaring hip hop music for an hour in the car was probably not the best way to treat this condition.

Anyway, they finally got there and drove up to the gate where the rather handsome 40ish parking attendant asked for the $10 to park the car. So Olivia rummaged around in her mammoth sized bag for her credit card that she threw in earlier that morning and casually handed it to the man. Then, to her horror, and as if in slow motion, she proceeded to watch him peel off a neatly folded panty liner from the back of her card!

Sinking low in her seat, she avoided the eyes of the handsome parking attendant as he passed back her credit card, along with the receipt and a pen, all wrapped neatly in the panty liner! Mortified, she opened it up to sign the receipt and found a business card reading...IF YOU SHOULD EVER NEED PERSONAL PROTECTION, PLEASE CALL BODYGUARD SERVICES. In pencil he had added the words: 'YOUR PAD, NOT MINE,' and a drawn smiley face.

Still unable to look at him, but grinning from ear to ear, Olivia sped away to screams from her daughter in the back. 'MUM!!! You are soooooo *embarrassing*! How are you ever going to get a boyfriend when you do stuff like that!?'

See, men don't have this problem. They don't have to carry such embarrassing items in their pockets, as they don't have to go through the same physical nonsense as a woman does.

Bit Of A Boob

Talking of physical nonsense – I hate strapless bras! As useful as they are when wearing a strapless top, feeling like they are slipping their way down to your waist and constantly having to heave them up all the livelong day is highly annoying. My friend had quite an embarrassing experience when she was out shopping one day.

She was wearing a strapless bra under a t-shirt (I have no idea why she didn't just wear a normal one) and was walking about all afternoon, attracting some strange glances.

She then entered River Island and lifted a top she quite liked from one of the racks and went to look at herself in the mirror. Just as she was about to hold the top in front of her to see if it suited, she noticed her nipples through her thin pink t-shirt. Confused at this, as most strapless bras are padded, she took a closer look in the mirror, and realised that her bra was around her waist! No wonder she was getting strange glances, it looked like she had four breasts!

One of my embarrassing bra experiences was with a filleted one. You know, the ones where you insert the extra little bit of help into your bra to give you that extra bit of bulk.

I was doing a stage combat class at theatre school and, as you can imagine, there is a lot of movement involved with that. It's all pretending to beat each other up without hurting one another (yeah right).

So after quite an energetic session, my friends and I went for lunch and as I was chatting away, I realised a couple of them were focusing on my waist. After a while I curiously glanced down to see what all the fuss was about, and my eyes nearly popped out of my head. One of my fillets had found its way out of my bra, travelled south and was tucked into the waist of my jeans with the top of it sticking in front of my top! As it was white, I made this pathetic excuse that it was a tissue, and that I had no idea as to how it got from my pocket to being tucked in at my waist...I don't think they bought it, probably because one boob was now bigger than the other.

That Bloated Feeling

And it's not only being worried if something will fall out of your clothing that women have to contend with, but trying to get into an item of clothing can be just as tough...and I'm not just talking about if you're too fat.

Women the world over suffer from bloated bellies due to eating stodgy foods such as white bread, pasta etc, but the most terrible thing about this, however, is that women aren't "allowed" to release their wind like men. So women have to hold in their, ahem, gas, and waddle around as if they are in first stage of pregnancy (more about this in another chapter!).

My good friend Anna thought that she would try on a smaller size pair of jeans one day whilst out shopping as she had lost some weight, although she was feeling a little bloated too. However, she managed to pull them on without too much hassle and admired herself in the changing room mirror, triumphant at the fact that she was in a smaller size jean.

But as she started to try and take the jeans off, panic struck - she couldn't get them off. No matter how hard she tugged, wriggled and yanked, they just weren't budging! It was like they were painted on!

Trying to remain calm but with her heartbeat increasing substantially, she opened the curtain and politely asked the woman in the next cubicle to help her undo the jeans...but no luck. The woman couldn't get them undone either. So then they called the assistant to see if she could help. By this time Anna had attracted a nice little audience in the changing room, and was now perspiring from embarrassment.

The assistant came in and after tugging with all her might at Anna's ass, those jeans were not for coming off.

So then the *manager* was called in to see if she could work any magic! After a few minutes of the manager grunting and gritting her teeth, pulling wildly at Anna's bottom, with both her feet practically on the wall, looking similar to a mountaineer, the jeans still didn't budge, and so they came to the conclusion that there was only one thing that they could do…cut her out of them!

So the manager took a stunned Anna out on to the *shop floor* (how mortifying!) and started to cut the jeans in front of an increasing number of shoppers/spectators. The manager cut them and Anna, whose heartbeat was so fast she was almost going into cardiac arrest, had enough room to manoeuvre them off (back in the changing room of course).

Anna has never returned to shop there, surprisingly enough.

If this was due to a fat thing, then I couldn't really say that this would just happen to a female - but it wasn't a fat issue – it was from being bloated from society (men) dictating that women should not be allowed to let their wind "break free", a thing that guys just don't have to put up with.

Yes, women, again, are bearing the brunt of God's anatomy choices – which escalates even more in the next chapter.

Chapter Four

Sex and the Shitty

Sex can be great for a woman, don't get me wrong, but along with the good, always comes some bad. I think that God definitely made sex an easier task for males than females. I mean, it's a wham-bam-thank-you-mam for guys, whereas for women it can be a bit more, 'Um, just a bit to the left...no, not quite....um, down a bit, no, not that far down....a bit to the right....nope....further up...oh forget it!'

I mean, women have no trouble finding the males "tool" to bring him pleasure, I mean its practically (sometimes literally) staring at us in the face. But a man trying to find the females? That can sometimes be like finding a needle in a haystack. Our "tool" is tiny. *I* barely know where it is. And some men should be forced to have a Sat Nav to locate it – 'TURN LEFT – DO A U-TURN –

STOP! YOU HAVE REACHED YOUR DESTINATION.' I mean, what was God thinking?

See, this is even more evidence that God must be a man, as he wasn't really bothered about our pleasure.

Even oral sex is more of a challenge. In an episode of Sex And The City, Samantha and her partner for the evening, are about to indulge in oral sex. The guy says, 'Come on, give me a little BJ, up and down a couple of times, you're done, it's easy!' with Samantha replying, 'Easy? You men have no idea what we're dealing with down there. Teeth placement, and jaw stress, and suction, and gag reflex, and all the while bobbing up and down, moaning and trying to breathe through our noses. Easy? Honey, they don't call it a job for nothin'!'

Faking It

Yes, it seems that women are on the losing team (again) when it comes to sex, and what makes it worse is that we make it even easier for men to have a trouble-free time of it. Women don't say anything in case we might offend!

Yes - it's those genes/chips again. I think that God placed "Don't Offend Men" chips inside women so that men can have all the pleasure they need and women will pretend to enjoy themselves when they are not. Because of this, men expect, and are indeed probably used to, women behaving like a female movie star in a sex scene – panting from the word go, together with the nails sinking into the guy's back.

What men quite often don't realise, however, is that a lot of the time, women are having a Meg Ryan moment like in 'When Harry Met Sally'. Whilst men feel that they have conquered Everest, the women are left lying unsatisfied, holding the covers over themselves, when they really should be holding an Oscar after

'I am just too damn talented for my own good'

the convincing performance they have just given.

I mean, why the hell are we compelled to be such good actresses? I'm telling you, it's that chip. We shouldn't make men feel so good about themselves when they get such an easy ride of it (no pun intended!). Yes, that gene needs to be conquered so men will get a little jolt – and that is certainly what one young gentleman needed.

A young woman I know of invited her date back to her apartment, alluding to what was going to be their first night of passion together. Soon they were getting down to business on the sofa in her dimly lit living room. They smoothly moved into the missionary position and off they went - well he did. This woman quickly became confused as to why this guy was thrusting back and forth and proclaiming how good it felt when he hadn't even put his "little friend" in "her area" yet. It was only after a few (short) minutes that the girl realised that he hadn't been making love to *her*, but to the *sofa!* And she never said anything! Apparently the sofa had very soft cushions.

But why do women do this? Can you imagine a woman - as ridiculously hard as this is - not even touching a man during sex and him not saying anything out of politeness?

Time To Pluck

And the preparation for a sexual encounter is enormous! We have to remove hair under the arms, legs, decide on which part of the world we would like our bikini area to represent – Hollywood or Brazil - take our magnifying glass out to pluck any little stray hairs that we didn't get, and then, *finally*, we choose the lingerie which make us look the hottest. Phew! It's hard work!

Whereas a man is ready for the "deed" anytime - anywhere. It's too unfair! There are no such thoughts of, 'Wait - what time of the month is it?' Or, 'Oh shit, I haven't shaved my legs!' when an impromptu rendezvous pops up on the horizon. They are allowed to be as hairy as they like and we just have to put up with it.

We just can't get away without having to remove our body hair, even if we don't mind it ourselves. Julia Roberts was almost crucified in the press when she waved at fans at a film premiere in a sleeveless dress and revealed her underarm hair to the world.

The First Time

The first time can be a bit of a nightmare for a female – no, not the *very* first time - although that is a bit of a nightmare too. For the male it's quite an enjoyable time I've heard, in contrast to a female's initiation into sex, which is more like, 'What the hell was that all about?!'

No, I'm talking about the first time with a new partner. The morning after the night before is always much less forgiving to a female than a male, especially if it is the first night you've spent together. Ok, sure, both sexes have horrendous morning breath, resulting in not much conversation when both waken up, but women have a lot more to conceal, even after all the preparation we have gone through: panda eyes, cellulite, stubbly legs, a bikini rash from being too thorough, and boobs not looking as big and as round without the chicken fillets that are now horrifyingly on the floor.

With all this to disguise, women have to make a terrifyingly quick dash to the nearest loo and do an emergency makeover. But instead of there being a flattering street lamp shining through the curtains into the bedroom, the morning after provides a "lovely" harsh sunlight to highlight all our flaws, making the journey to the loo all the more daunting.

A girl I know of had a bit of a disaster in this type of situation. Wakening up and presuming that she looked a fright after a night of passion with her new boyfriend, she quietly started to tiptoe her way to the ensuite toilet whilst the guy was still asleep, in a bid to pretend to him that she looks as great in the morning as she always does.

However, on the way, she stood on his pet dog's squeaky toy, which not only wakened the boyfriend, but his dog too. The little terrier bolted in at lightening speed and launched straight at her, knocking her off her feet, head first into a leather beanbag, leaving her bare behind and everything else on display. It wasn't quite the vision that she was hoping her boyfriend would awaken to!

Love Vibrations

However, there is a way of women receiving pleasure and not having to worry about exhibiting all her "bits" to peering eyes – the Vibrator! Yes, women came up with a little creation of their own, God. Women can just switch this little device on whenever they want to make them all aquiver. They can control it, point it in the right direction and make it last as long as need be, all without the phallus's ego being deflated, and not a Sat Nav in sight.

Yes, the vibrator is something that perhaps God did not count on being created, with women not having to rely on men for their sexual enjoyment ('Damn,' I bet God and his male "soul mates" said, 'women are becoming too independent!'). I think guys are a little shocked at times when they realise that women don't need them as much as they think they do.

Jacqueline Gold transformed the Ann Summers chain into a multi-million pound business after realising women wanted to buy sex toys. At first her father's business associates (male I presume) told her that it would never work as, 'Women just aren't interested in sex.' Well, I think they were forced to eat their words. Yes, women went sex toy and sexy lingerie galore with their **WOMEN ONLY** Tupperware-style parties. Aw, I think the poor guys felt left out in the cold.

The Bastard

But no wonder a lot of women have now become accustomed to using their little vibrating friend as opposed to the real thing, as there is no heartache involved. Now, as a modern woman, I realise that women can have no strings attached sex like men, and if the general consensus between two grown adults is that, 'This is just for fun,' then that's fine. But it's when porkies come into the equation that causes the problem – and men are the greatest culprits here.

Yes, it's the reassuring "Romeo" sweet-talking his way into bed with a woman who is looking for more than just an orgasm. Ensuring her that she is beautiful, and that he *really* wants to see her again whilst overloading her with alcohol, he then does a runner the next day. Then there's the guy who does the dirty and two-times a woman and uses the excuse, 'I'm a guy, I'm weak.' Now perhaps they are weak and pathetic when it comes to sex. God probably made them this way so that they think that they can have their cake and eat it too.

'Mm, come to mama!'

But be aware: having our hearts broken can lead to gorging on too much chocolate and that can lead to dangerous consequences. Yes, we mustn't succumb to too much comfort eating, this will only add to God's plan to give us more cellulite, hence making our self-esteem even less, which, in the end, will make us more vulnerable to end up in bed with another bastard!

The Stud

Another shitty thing that women have to endure is when a man can't take no for an answer (probably due to the overload of testosterone, or as I like to call it: assholeness). I'm sure we've all been there when no matter how cold you are being towards your predator, he just doesn't take the hint to buzz off.

As if women didn't have enough to deal with, what with mending broken hearts, trying to get rid of unwanted body hair, but we also have to try and rid ourselves of unwanted attention from males. I have actually noticed that God must have given similar genes/chips to all of the species on this planet, and so it's not only human females that have this shit to deal with.

Take the nature programmes for example. How often have you seen the male lion trying to mount the female, and the female desperately trying to run away, but the male lion doesn't take the hint? Or the pigeons you have sometimes watched and fed whilst sitting on a park bench, with the male pigeon all of a sudden strutting his stuff and ruffling his feathers before he flaps his wings and pounces on the unsuspecting female. All it needs is a leather jacket and a Harley.

I wish men would understand that this kind of behaviour really doesn't impress females. I always laugh at guys who roar around in their "sports" cars with an ear-splitting exhaust, believing that all the females will just swoon as they zoom by. Well, reality check please to all men who do this: women are really just thinking you are quite pathetic and its what I personally call SPS – Small Penis Syndrome.

Double Standards!!

Yes, God made guys want to go out and hunt for sex, made women so polite that she won't say if he's rubbish in bed, and then the males are deemed studs the more women they sleep with. What a perfect world he was creating for the guys! Isn't that even more evidence that God is one of the blokes?

It's really unfair and such double standards how a woman is branded a slut for being with a lot of men, but a guy is deemed cool for being with a lot of women!! God must have placed genes/chips in humanity to think that it is shameful for women to express themselves sexually, but also placed "Boastful" genes in men - so that guys could get to have all the fun and that women were supposed to have none.

Yes, I think they thought they had it all figured out, as most males prefer their women to be almost virginal when they get together with them, and the thought that *their* woman has "been" with other men, is too much to handle.

A lot of religions and cultures see a woman as impure if she has had any sexual relations before marriage…but no mention of how "impure" a man is if he has had pre-marital sex! I mean, think about why women get married in a WHITE wedding dress – to show to the world that she is pure and virginal, yet is the man expected to wear white?

The word Virgin is the root form of the Latin noun Virgo meaning: "A maiden, young WOMAN", and "A virgin, a sexually intact WOMAN." Why mainly women??!! I wonder what gender created that definition?

Women have been made to feel dirty for their sexual desires - and it was all started by men (probably stemming from the male assistants in heaven who encouraged God to give women the harder physical life).

And on the subject of double standards, how is it that hardly anybody bats an eyelid when a fifty-something year old male has a twenty-something female hanging off his arm? They can happily stroll around town without too much attention, perhaps just the odd glance or two. But when an older woman has a younger male at her side, there is almost shock horror!

There have been horrible headlines and comments in newspapers and magazines referring to Ashton Kutcher and Demi Moore's union: 'MOTHER AND SON GO OUT TO DINNER.' *'Ashton's mother is looking nice, now he should go out and get himself a real girlfriend.'* And, *'She should get her hair cut to make her look younger.'*

Ok, I do admit that the norm is usually a younger female with an older male, which is so infuriating, because God has done it again. Think about it: most women tend to go for males older than themselves. This starts from a very early age, usually the teenage years - a girl will usually date an older guy – and it continues. So, don't you see? Men are always guaranteed to have a youthful woman on their arm, a little bit of eye candy. And we are stuck with falling for the old geezers as they have the maturity that we crave.

Blind Date

Another thing that is harder for the females when it comes to dating is that men tend not to look much deeper than the skin we are in, making it tough if we are having an off day. Whereas guys have it all sewn up as women have more of an ability to look past what's on the outside and

73

try and see the "person" on the inside. So a guy with a not so pleasing appearance can triumph on a date if he reveals his personality and cracks a few funnies. Whereas most women wouldn't have a chance if they looked under par but were hilarious also. I've heard, so many times, friends of mine saying their date wasn't so great looking but 'He was so sweet!' So they decide to get together again, with most of my friends really pleased that they have found someone nice.

However I have heard so many guys that have slated their "mates" if they go on a date with a "dog" without being the least bit interested if she was a nice person or not.

Take Note

So, God basically made it easier for men to enjoy themselves in the sexual encounters and dating game area, and so us women have to fight this "Don't Offend Men" and "Ashamed" chip. If a woman wants to have lots of sexual partners, then she should be able to shout out loud and proud to the world just as much as a guy! And if men find the honesty difficult to take when the "Don't

Offend Men" gene is curbed, who cares? That's just a tough learning curve that they are just going to have to go through.

One of my girlfriends and I recently had a conversation with a young guy about girls being polite in bed. He told us that his girlfriend of 2 ½ years has *never* faked it. My friend and I both looked at each other and smiled at his naiveté - we had to tell him the truth. It is an understatement to say his expression changed from triumphant to that of a very stunned and worried looking young man. Bless!

So, I thought that I would write a couple of notes to both men and women so that hopefully relations can be improved:

Note to Men: If a woman starts to pant like a dog the moment you touch her, this is not real (unless her hormones are *really* playing havoc with her). This means that you should really change tactics and re-think your 4-4-2 formation to perhaps a 3-3-4 (Yes, I thought I'd incorporate some football talk to get your attention).

Note to Women: Fight those chips! Be proud of your sexual desires! And make sure that you get what you want out of an encounter in the bedroom. Your honesty will cause your partner to probably get a shock in the beginning, as you lie silently until you actually feel like making a noise, but it will be better in the long run. Think of it as like training a pet to do things properly. Another memorable quote from Sex And The City's Samantha sums up what I mean: "When I RSVP to a party, I make it my business to come."

Now if men and women take those points on board, then I think the world will be a much grander and more pleasurable place.

Chapter Five

A Taboo Subject

This subject is usually a taboo one, well, at least when it comes to women. But ladies, lets be honest with each other, we all do it. Yes, I'm talking about farting (and pooing). Even the Queen must do it! 'Philip!' the Queen might say, 'Can you pass me some more loo roll?!' And, 'Oops, pardon me Philip.' And supermodels! They must be guilty of the odd break of wind or two, especially if it is true that some of them take laxatives to stay thin. Note to men: sorry for ruining any unrealistic fantasy that beautiful women don't do such things.

Unfair Advantage

Men seem to be able to express themselves easier in this area. Yes, it's those genes/chips again. This time God placed the "Loud & Proud" one in men so they could shout out to the world about it, and that they would be appalled at any woman who joined in. Yet God never bothered with this gene for women, but still had the nerve to give us plenty of wind to break.

You see, men and women digest food in the exact same way, so there's no sensible biological reason why women should "parp" any less than men. Yes, I believe that, instead, God gave us the "Embarrassed To Break Wind" chip so that, of course, men wouldn't have to put up with any disgusting aromas, making their lives even more pleasant than that of a female. I mean, how incredibly unfair!

Even peeing is easier for men. I mean, guys can pee in a public place, no problem. They just whip their little friend out, do the deed, and after a little shake, they're done. For women it's a whole different ball game. We have to strip half naked, squat like a rugby player, try not to dribble down our legs, try to avoid peeing on our pants that are down around our ankles, frantically shake our toosh to dry ourselves, whilst at the same time, trying to rotate our heads an impossible 360 degrees just to make sure that nobody is checking out our bare ass!

A female friend of mine was peeing behind a bush once and got stung in her bum from a bee! The injustice of what women have to go through!

Breaking The Ice (or should that be wind?)

Another of my friends started a new job in an office a while ago and on her first day she went to the local pub for lunch with some of her colleagues in a bid to get to know them better. As she was waiting for the lift to arrive at her floor, two of her male colleagues stood with her, but they were all having a little bit of an awkward silence. Thoughts raced through her head of what she could say, what interesting conversation she could strike up to break this silence. One of her colleagues must have been having the same thoughts, only to come to the conclusion of there was nothing to talk about, so instead - he broke wind. And apparently it wasn't subtle.

Both the male colleagues collapsed into hysterics whilst she just stared at the ceiling not knowing where to look.

The Great Escape

Yes, this is the difference between the designs of the two sexes. God made women embarrassed about the subject and he made men want to brag about it.

'Oh no! He heard me!'

'PARP'

There is no doubt that women, especially when initially dating a guy, would rather die than break wind in front of their man (no wonder there are so many women with bloated bellies!). Yes, when there is an imminent current of air travelling your way, it's usually a case of squeezing your ass and all of your internal organs together as tightly as possible to prevent any possible escape and praying that your partner will leave the room immediately, so you can let your wind break free and your organs can return to their natural positions. And a lot of women become an expert in "silent" farts – letting their air escape *very* slowly and carefully, monitoring every movement, so their partner remains unaware of their doings.

However, one night my friend, who had been dating her boyfriend for a few months, unexpectedly let her guard down. She was asleep with her legs curled up and her boyfriend was peacefully watching the telly. Then all of a sudden a loud blast of wind escaped from her, which was so loud, she woke herself up! 'Huh!' her boyfriend gasped, 'You just *farted*!' This was the first time he had heard such a noise emanating from her body. It is quite an understatement to say that she was quite embarrassed and pretended to go back to sleep very quickly!

I mean, it is so unfair that men can get away with producing extremely offensive gas from their bottom, but it is totally frowned upon when a woman does this.

Oh Shit!

Yes, the amount of shit (quite literally) that men can get away with compared to women is unreal.

One of my partner's immediate female family members, (I shan't embarrass her by naming her!) and her boyfriend, were at a house party once and she really needed to do a "number two" and so decided to go to the loo, as she could not hold this monstrosity in any longer (she must have been really desperate, as she *never* does a "number two" in public).

After being relieved, she was horrified at the repugnant smell that she had produced and knew that it was only a matter of time for it to waft in to the very near living room - so she had to think quick. She marched straight over to her partner and quietly instructed him to go to the bathroom - immediately. Confused at being ordered to go to the toilet when he didn't need, he asked why. She explained that he was to go into the loo for a few moments and pretend that he had just done the shit that she had just done and take the blame for the smell.

Dutifully bound, he did what he was told and got her off the hook and everyone at the party made fun of her partner for the horrendous scent that filtered through. She is eternally grateful to her long-suffering partner, who still gets flak from the other partygoers to this day.

A Public Performance

Yes, women are usually a lot more discreet when it comes to toilet related activities. I mean, don't get me wrong - women usually enjoy being in public loos together. We share make-up tips, talk about guys, have a little gossip, and are especially good at helping out a friend in need by passing a loo roll underneath to the next cubicle when a lady has discovered there isn't any.

However, one of my friends has IBS and gets embarrassed at the noise her bowel makes when she is "eliminating her toxins" in public loos, and so would rather be on her own, instead of making it a social event. She even tries to disguise the racket her bowel produces: sometimes with a cough, or pretending that she is blowing her nose and, more often or not, waits until the women in the cubicles next to her flush the pan before she "lets loose".

On this one occasion, it was just herself and another woman in a posh powder room at a business function she was attending, and it was so quiet, you could hear a pin drop. My friend hovered over the pan (she can't sit down on a public pan as it freaks her out that there has been thousands of bare asses on it before her), in a similar position to a skier travelling down a slope. Realising that no fake cough or sneeze could disguise what she was about to unload, she decided to hold off until the woman exited the toilet.

However, the woman was taking an age to wash her hands. 'C'mon!' she silently pleaded, 'Leave!' With the intentions of her bowel becoming more and more imminent, and the lengthy time this woman was taking to lather her hands in the Molton Brown handwash, her thighs started shaking from the squat like pose that she was holding. But then she had a light bulb above her head moment. Realising that she wouldn't be able to hold off for the woman to leave, she would "let loose" when she turned the hand dryer on! 'That ought to do the trick,' she thought. She then heard the tap being turned off. 'Halleluiah! Any second now!' she jubilantly whispered, with her thighs and bowel not being able to hold on for much longer.

Then, almost as if it was in slow motion, she heard the woman bang on the hand-dryer button, and she finally set free an array of horrific "parp" sounds into the echo friendly pan, finishing with a reverberating big "plop". 'Ah relief!.......but hang on a minute,' she thought, 'I don't hear the hand dryer.' The hand dryer was broken! The only hot air that had been expelled was from her rear end!

Shocked and disillusioned with her failed attempt to disguise her anal din, her thighs gave in and she collapsed onto the pan, with the sound of hurried footsteps exiting from the toilet.

Now, from what I've heard, guys just go into a public loo and don't care what they have to do and how loud it's going to be. They don't seem to bother about volume control or scent. In fact, the louder and stronger the better, in their case. I suppose it shows more "manliness".

I actually (and unfortunately) experienced this, first hand, the other week. I accidentally and horrifyingly went in to the men's loo in a supermarket and was wondering what was happening in the cubicle next to me. It sounded as if there was a bear in it – there were groans and everything! How different from a women's loo!

Women try so hard to conceal every noise and smell! However this was not possible for yet another lady too.

One day in a train station loo, I, and several others were waiting in a queue for a little girl and her Mother to come out of the only cubicle. All of a sudden the little sweet girl's voice said, 'This is a good day today Mummy, your poo is coming out quick so we'll make the train.' Kids, don't you just love 'em?

Poisonous Gas

Yes, it really is difficult to control one's self when you have IBS. And it is also particularly difficult to control one's self when you have food poisoning.

Yes, my brother Mark had quite an enjoyable time after he ate some bad fish. Ok, yes he was in pain, hallucinating a little, and was slightly confused at what the Pepto Bismol bottle meant by "stools", but he managed to alleviate his symptoms easily and take pleasure in engulfing those around him with his strongly scented gas (that is a serious understatement!).

Yes, God certainly made it easier for men than women in this area of life. I mean, guys have farting competitions with each other as they watch football on TV and drink their beers. I've even heard that they sometimes set their fart alight by holding a lighter next to their bottoms!!

However, if a female "parps" in front of her other female friends, there is a stunned silence, a red face, and a very sincere apology.

A Little Draughty

There is also a different orifice in the female body that air can be unexpectedly expelled from. Yes, the Vagina - a whole other different type of fart.

A lady I know, was attending a weekly yoga class with her boyfriend a while back, with the aim of reducing her stress and becoming "in tune" with her body and soul. And on this particular week, it was only the two of them who had turned up for the class, which they thought was great - that meant more personal attention!

However, they still found some of the positions quite difficult to grasp - the Garudasana, the Utkatasana, the Matsyasana – just trying to pronounce the words were difficult enough, never mind trying to get into the correct position! However, it wasn't until this lady got into the Sarvangasana pose - lying on the top half of your back with your legs and bum straight up in the air so that your legs are in a vertical line from the ceiling to the floor - that things got interesting.

They were told to hold this pose for approximately five minutes and, even though it was slightly tricky, this lady felt like she had really got the hang of it. Feeling that she was "in the moment" and with the gentle music on in the background, it felt like all her stresses of the day were just melting away and her blood pressure must have been perfect.

After the five minutes were up, they were then told to relax and to gently come out of the pose by slowly lowering their legs to the floor. By this time she was in a "deep spiritual state" with the "Om's" and mantras emanating from the CD player. She started to lower her legs at the requested leisurely pace, but then all of a sudden let out a succession of massive fart sounds as well!

Her "deep spiritual state" quickly turned into a state of shock horror, and her leisurely paced legs crashed to the floor at lightening speed! 'Oh, my, God! Please tell me that did not just happen?' she excruciatingly thought to herself. Then another one came out as she quickly tried to get into another position. Her perfect blood pressure was now sky high! This was so embarrassing, with the main reason being that the "farts" weren't coming from her bottom, they were coming from…her vagina! Yes, it's the welcome FANNY FARTS. And she had absolutely no control! The boisterous air just kept powering out, no matter how hard she clenched her pelvic muscles, teeth, toes, fists,

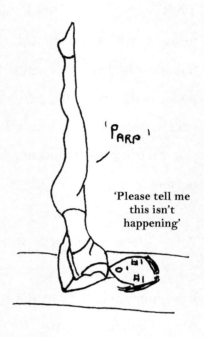

'P_{ARP}'

'Please tell me this isn't happening'

ass, *anything* that could squeeze together to stop it!

Sweating and shaking from the sheer disbelief that this was happening, she looked round to see the teacher's reaction. He was looking confused as to where the noises were coming from, so she quickly took some initiative, looked at her boyfriend and blamed him. 'Rob!' she said in a very stern manner, 'Stop it!' with Rob's mouth falling open with shock at her sheer audacity.

However, it became obvious that she was the culprit, as the "farts" kept coming for some while and so she had to own up. The teacher just gave an awkward smile and kind of just continued with the class.

The most frustrating and embarrassing thing, however, was probably the fact that the teacher thought they were actual farts that she was doing. But how could she have ever explained that they were coming from her vagina? I think that would have just made the situation all the more cringe-worthy.

Yes, I'm sure that the possibility of "parping" out of our vaginas was all in God's master plan to bring him yet even more comic relief. I'm sure God thought it was highly amusing when deciding to leave this option open so women would have not just one orifice in their lower body where wind can power out, but two! And to give us the same amount of gas to expel as men but give us a chip that makes us feel embarrassed about it is just cruel!

Well, unfortunately for us ladies, God's cruelness continues, as the next chapter proves.

Chapter Six

Expecting Company?

It can be a wonderful and exciting time when you find out you are expecting a baby. You celebrate, surprise everyone, look forward to the new arrival... but then soon after, when you're feeling as sick as a parrot, the whole reality of it can sink in.

Women have to sacrifice a whole lot more than men during this time...yes, there's that unfair thing again. Men produce a bit of sperm. There. That's it. That is their part over and done with. And they even get to have a good time whilst doing so. Then they just sit back and put their feet up. Women, on the other hand, have to put their jobs/career on hold and give up alcohol for 9 months - no, actually, it's longer than that if you want to breastfeed. Yes, if you are going to do the recommended

6 months feeding, it could end up being nearer fifteen months without even so much as a tiny slurp of a Cosmopolitan or a glass of Chablis!! What is up with that God??? (*How on earth will I cope?!*)

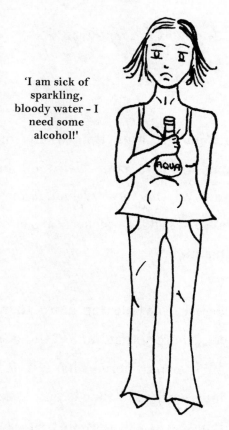

'I am sick of sparkling, bloody water - I need some alcohol!'

Yes, whilst we sit being teetotal with an enlarged tum, sipping a sparkling water with a daring slice of lemon on a Saturday night, we have to endure watching the other half have a merry old time, flashing us a drunken smile as they down their fourth glass of vino.

Body Alterations

Yes, being a mum-to-be is tough and can make your job even more challenging. Lack of concentration, forgetfulness, morning sickness, constipation, and the constant peeing in the first stages of pregnancy, can seriously interfere with your daily schedule of meetings and power-point presentations.

And why is it that they call it *morning* sickness when it happens all the livelong day? This unfortunate state of nausea is thought to be caused by chemical changes the body is going through – yes, again, God is responsible for those "chemicals". The chemical changes also seem to produce an enhanced sense of smell, which is why a woman can be crazy for coffee and then when pregnant, be completely repulsed by it! Wonderful, we can't even drink our favourite beverage now!

Another (embarrassing) matter during early pregnancy is an increase in gas – and I'm not talking about the stuff you put in your car. Apparently, during early pregnancy, progesterone relaxes the smooth muscle tissue of the intestine, slowing digestion and leading to a build-up of gas. I mean, why does this *have* to happen?? I swear God was designing all this to give him a laugh, so if he was ever feeling low all he would have to do is pin-point a pregnant lady on earth from up above and have a good old giggle.

And then there's the mood swings, similar to PMT. Now granted, this hormonal change in a woman is perhaps not too pleasant for our partners either, not knowing whether to fear or pity us – but well, who the hell cares? Do they have a human being growing inside of *them*?

Extreme MakeUnder

Something else to then look forward to during pregnancy is perhaps more spots (the skin apparently gets oilier) or brown patches on your face. Apparently a lot of women develop Chloasma (increased pigmentation) on their face and body. Now, this could have been a nice thing to happen during pregnancy, kind of like a free fake tan. But no, God was obviously going for the comic effect once again, and so instead of developing an even all over glow, we develop patches which look shit….and, of course, not forgetting about the bout of acne to go. Ah, God, don't you just love him?

Hair then starts to sprout from new orifices too. Some women get hair on their belly, a moustache, even hair on their nipples (*what the hell?*). And women are advised not to dye their hair when pregnant just to be on the safe side, so we also have to let the grey locks start to show their true colours to the world.

The next fact that I learnt about pregnancy shocked me quite a bit – women's feet can grow! Yes, due to the extra bodily fluid swimming around, not only is your ass and boobs going to get bigger (I must admit that I don't mind the boobs becoming larger), so apparently will your feet. Yes, a lot of the fluid finds its way straight to the old tootsies, increasing our shoe size by one or even two sizes – with the possibility of them staying larger after the birth!

So let me re-cap so far: what pregnancy will create is a forgetful, constipated and cranky woman with a moustache, acne, hairy nipples, and big clown feet. Mm, puts a whole new light on the "glow" of a pregnant lady.

'Ok, this is just taking the piss'

I mean, was God high when he was designing what women will go through when with child??? And I haven't even mentioned the haemorrhoids and varicose veins!

Mm, the pictures of Demi Moore and a whole other host of celebs posing whilst heavily pregnant must seriously have been airbrushed!

All that a mum-to-be has to suffer is ridiculous, especially as a dad-to-be goes through NOTHING! Yes, God knew what he was doing there for all his male companions.

Too Posh To Push

So now your ass is wider, your belly has been stretched beyond all belief, and your boobs are giving Jordan a run for her money, it's now time to pop the baby out - but how?

Years ago, you had no option but to push and shove until your veins in your head popped. However, nowadays things have changed. A lot of women are now opting for a C-section to avoid the "stretching" effect and the pain of a vaginal birth. Some people think that the "too posh to push" brigade are missing out on the natural birthing experience and that it is a lot more dangerous having a caesarean. I think I may be with the vaginal birth as opposed to the C- section. Sure C-sections can be life saving, but I think that is what they should be used for only, as painful as giving birth is!

Phew, getting a little too serious there. But what a choice from God eh? 'Yes madam, would you like to squeeze the human being out of your vagina or have your abdomen cut open to remove it?' I have to say, I've had better choices to make in life.

Au Naturale

So, if deciding on going natural via the birth canal, women are then spun into a quandary of what their birth plan should include. Should they have the pain killing drugs? Or should they opt for just gas and air? Is that even natural?? I'm confused! There are just too many things to think about when having a baby.

Some women nowadays are having natural water births at home and using a Tens machine as pain relief. However not all women are quite on the same path. I heard of a woman who said to the nurse, 'Are you kidding? Going natural to me means having no make-up on, now GIVE ME THE DRUGS!'

Something else that isn't quite natural is the position that women get into to give birth. I mean, would you lie down to go to the toilet? No! So why the hell are women put in a bed and told to lie down to push a human being out of them? Gravity alone will tell you that is crazy. I'm guessing that this was started by a male, in the beginning of time, fresh with the knowledge that God gets his kicks from seeing women suffer. I'd love to see the expression on a male's face if they were told to lie down whilst they went to move their bowels. They would think that person was off their head!

Congratulations! It's A......Poop?

Talking of moving bowels, not only is giving birth probably the most painful experience that anyone could go through, it is also a little undignified.

A woman I know was pushing so hard whilst giving birth that she pooped right in front of everyone. I think her partner got quite a shock, as he thought she had just given birth to the baby! I have heard from a good source (a child bearing woman) that this is a major problem for women in labour - trying to push the baby out whilst trying to hold a poo in, is really tricky! No wonder they give some women an enema before they start to push!

This whole palaver is out of order, God! I mean, its bad enough having people stare at your vagina for hours upon hours, waiting on a little human to pass through it, without then doing a great big poop right in front of them! I mean, talk about losing your dignity.

I think an episode of Scrubs, the US hospital comedy series, sums up the true birthing experience. When J.D. (the doctor) is with a woman in labour he thinks to himself, 'I think childbirth has been way too romanticized.' He goes on to say to the woman, 'You'll fart, poop, pee, and scream, all in front of ten complete strangers, all of whom are staring intently at your vagina, which, by the way, has an 80 per cent chance of tearing.' The woman then turns to her husband and says, 'You do it!'

Blood Bath

If you have not had an "easy" birth, trying to get out of bed to go and shower without it looking like something out of a horror movie is generally quite difficult.

My boyfriend's sister, Lesley, couldn't quite make it to the hospital toilet without it looking like a Quentin Tarantino movie had just been shot there, after she had torn and delivered the placenta naturally after having her first child. There were pools of blood everywhere, and apparently it took a while to stop (I think I may be getting a little turned off from having a baby, I think I may suggest to my boyfriend that we adopt!).

Yes, the aftereffects of giving birth can be quite gruesome and you may need some stitching to, well, restore your "area".

Another lady I know, who tore when giving birth, said the midwife commented on her newly darned genitalia, saying, 'Aw, you look just like a patchwork quilt.'

Today's Special Is......

So, after you have had your embroidery work done and have lost some more of your dignity, as you are now sitting on a rubber ring, there is yet another decision you have to make relating to your pregnancy. No, not, 'Should I give my baby the MMR jab?' Or, 'When should I return to work?' No, no. Here comes the choice of whether or not to eat.... the Placenta!!

Now granted, a lot of cultures believe in eating the placenta to give them nutrition, easing post-natal depression. Or some women, such as Penny Lancaster (partner of Rod Stewart), take it home, bury it and grow a tree. And other women use it to paint pictures and display them as art.

All of these, I can kind of see a point to. I suppose they are symbols that help the woman to always remember her pregnancy, and to always be a part of it. All that does sound kind of cool and spiritual, and I could maybe get on board with burying it and growing a tree.

But I have to say that I don't think I could face consuming it and, considering that eating the placenta seems to be a minority deed, I think that most women would agree that they have had better menus to choose from. 'Yes madam, our special today is the afterbirth that has exited from your vagina, now would you like that with a side of veg?'

After all that palaver, women then have to contend with milk pouring from their breasts and being hooked up to a pump to express their milk, similar in style to a dairy cow. And then to top the whole giving birth experience off, along comes the joint stiffness, feeling like you've just fought a round with Mike Tyson.

Time To Get Back In Shape

After pregnancy there are your exercises you must do. No, I'm not talking about huffing and puffing in the gym to lose the baby weight - I'm talking about your pelvic exercises. Yes, not only do you have a milkshake-to-go from your breasts, a ready-made meal exiting from your vagina, you now have some bladder weakness too. Just what the hell is going on??? I thought it was only the baby that was supposed to wear nappies! Yes, you thought that the weakness was only to happen during your pregnancy but your vagina is still leaking away. Doctors, however, say that this shouldn't last long after birth, only a "few weeks". Oh, well that's all right then, if we are only going to pee our pants for just a little while, then I don't know what I was worrying about! (yes, I am being sarcastic)

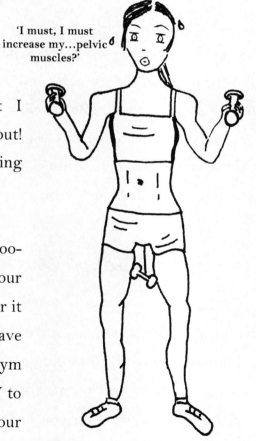

'I must, I must increase my...pelvic muscles?'

Apparently, the sooner you start your exercises the sooner it will go away. I have even seen a little gym style weight on TV to place inside your vagina so you can 'WORK THOSE PELVIC

MUSCLES!' I mean, I've heard of increasing your biceps with weights, but this is just getting ridiculous! I can't exactly imagine a lot of women flexing those muscles and offering people a feel to see how strong they are.

Sad But True

It is an understatement to say that there is a hell of a lot going on with a woman's body after birth, but what is probably the most awful, is post-natal depression.

Your body has just gone through a mammoth task – I mean, you have just produced a human being!! Yes, as if the pregnancy and giving birth wasn't enough to cope with, we then get laden with major depression. And even though all you want to do is just get on with looking after your baby, there is a dark cloud hanging over you, and unfortunately you can't quite connect with your newborn. And whilst you are struggling to cope with all the turbulent emotions going on inside of you, your man is happily cradling the baby, blissfully unaware of your feelings. This is definitely no laughing matter.

However, ladies, I have heard that one theory as to why women get this condition is because they have lost so much Omega 3 during the pregnancy. Omega 3, in particular, is found in the emotional centre of the brain (it's really handy having a scientist as my partner!) and when you are pregnant, the baby "absorbs" a lot of this from you. The result is that your emotional centre is starved.

So my top tip to make the whole pregnancy thing a little easier for women the world over would be to top up on your Omega 3 afterwards. It might just make a difference!

So it seems that pregnancy can be looked at in 2 ways: it's either a blessing or a curse. Would women rather have men go through all the pain and sacrifice? I'm sure some would. But then again, some would never give up the extraordinary and wonderful bonding experience that carrying your child inside of you for 9 months gives you.

Whichever way you look at it, I still think that God should have made it a tad less painful, we could still drink alcohol without it affecting the baby, and our boobs should stay inflated instead of shrinking back down!

Chapter Seven

Having It All

This is where things really get tricky for a woman – being a working mother. So far, after the pain of giving birth, then trying to cope with the sleep deprivation, changing the hundreds of dirty nappies and having your nipples sucked 'til they're sore, has been tough enough, without then having to work out how you can fit in having a career as well.

The Guilt Trip (or should that be "chip"?)

Now I must admit that I am keen on getting married and having children, and having a career…but phew! What a lot on one's plate! There is a constant thought going round in my, and I'm sure several million other women's heads of, 'How can I balance trying to be an award winning businesswoman of the year and being a super-duper mum at the same time?' It's almost impossible - and I think that God is responsible for this.

I believe that God must have implanted a little "Guilt" chip inside women, so that "having it all" feels like mission impossible. I'm sure his hope is that women will just give up on the dream, and end up staying at home to do all the housework, hence letting men away from having to share the chores.

I mean, men seem to be able to have it all ok. They can have the great job, the beautiful wife and children, the recreational time to do stupid dumb immature stuff with their friends (such as play computer games and actually believe that they are really driving that fast car on the screen, or that they really are a multi-talented, multi-millionaire footballer playing for Real Madrid) without even batting an eyelid. This is because they have no "Guilt" chip.

Women, on the other hand, have this little inner tug of war that constantly won't let them enjoy themselves when they are away from their kids.

In an episode of Desperate Housewives, Lynette swaps roles with her husband after years of boredom with being a housewife. However, after landing a top job that she is finding both challenging and exciting, she can't help but feel unbelievably guilty about the long hours she is putting in, which is preventing her from spending quality time with her young kids. After a lot of persuasion with her boss, she eventually gets a crèche at work and is able to see her youngest offspring more - lessening her guilt.

Ok, this is maybe fiction, but could you imagine a guy going to all that trouble?

Even the Spice Girls have suffered due to this guilt. The feisty ladies cut short their world reunion tour because of their mini spices. Victoria Beckham was quoted as saying, 'We have children, they need to get back to school…our families are our priorities.' What chance have regular women got if even the Spice Girls can't have it all?

But even if a woman has no children, it's still a tough world out there for us to succeed.

Stitched Up

Digressing a little, another thing that God "fixed" for the guys is that both men *and* women overestimate the intelligence of males and underestimate that of the females!!!

Yes, recent research by Professor Adrian Furnham, shows that the male ego tends to exaggerate cleverness whilst females seem happy to play dumb. Apparently society has been set-up to think that men are cleverer - which obviously is going to be more beneficial for men in the workplace.

So it looks like us women have been placed with even more faulty genes/chips. This one must be the "Play Dumb" chip and men have been given the "Asshole" one.

Think about how women tend to be criticised for their driving by males and you see that this is true: 'Women can't drive,' 'Tsk, typical woman driver.' Yet car insurance is so much more expensive for a young male as opposed to a young female, as the males have more accidents!!

What men tend to think of as "good" driving is probably about going fast. Well, I tend to think – and I'm sure you will agree - that "good" driving is about being safe. So you see, we are actually the more intelligent ones here, but being made to feel as though we are not.

And think about how men usually like their women to look. The pose from the gorgeous girl on the typical lads mag is usually one of dumbness: pouting lips with the finger in the mouth and eyes wide open with the expression of, 'I don't have a brain.' And we are quite happy to pose like this to make the males feel superior!

I think this relates to how men tend not to like women being funny. Men usually prefer to be the ones cracking the jokes and have the woman just sit and look pretty and shake with laughter at their "amusing" stories. Think about the ratio of female comedians compared to male ones and that says it all really.

Here Comes The......Ridiculousness

Yes, the "Play Dumb" gene has been with us for quite some time. Think of weddings: the bride is just expected to sit and look pretty and not say a word and let all the men make the speeches. And the vicar/priest used to pronounce a couple, 'Man and Wife,' after they got wed. I'm sorry, man and **WIFE???** What, are we no longer a woman after we get married? We are just a wife?!

In fact, in the eighteenth and nineteenth-century, the woman's separate identity was **nullified** at her marriage, and she was incorporated into the identity of her husband!! And all her property was passed to the control of her husband too!! But, I have noticed that since "Girl Power" a lot of clergymen are now pronouncing couples, 'Husband and Wife.' Now that's more like it.

However, even though women are "allowed" to hold on to their property nowadays when getting married, and clerics are being a tad more PC, things aren't altogether so different.

I mean, what about the whole taking the husband's name absurdity? It seems that women's identities are still being stolen in the twentieth-first-century!!

Now, granted, perhaps some women dislike their surname enough to change it to their hubby's, but why should this be *expected* of a bride?

Another ludicrous thing about weddings are the traditional wedding vows - it is only the woman who says the "obey" part. Another obvious indication that God and all his male assistants wanted women to feel inferior to men. And what is the ridiculousness of a man nowadays (and indeed ever!) asking a lady's father for her hand in marriage? I mean, how degrading. It feels like you're on sale with the transaction nearing completion at the beginning of the ceremony when the cleric asks: 'Who gives this woman to this man?' With the father of the bride replying: 'I do.' I mean we're not property!! How many "Asshole" genes have males had from God?!!

However, there is one good marriage related thing going on for women in the twenty-first century. No, not because we don't have to hand over all our belongings to our other half, or that we don't completely have to have our individuality exterminated, but because we can now love them and leave them if **WE** choose. It wasn't until 1857 that a woman could initiate divorce proceedings. Before then, it was only a man that could! Because of course, how could a woman possibly know what she wants?

Corrupt A-Gender

Digressing a little further, what is also quite worrying, and another part of God's and his soul mates' plan to make women feel inferior to men, is that most people have an image of a male when asked what gender automatically pops into their head, when asked to think of a person in an intelligent profession. I have made a small list of careers for you to see for yourself just how strong those genes in us are. Be aware of what sex instantly pops into your head:

DOCTOR

SCIENTIST

SURGEON

PSYCHIATRIST

I bet most of you thought of a male – and if you didn't, well done, you must be fighting the "Play Dumb" gene!

Stone Me!

Getting back to women trying to have it all, most people seem to think that during the Stone Age, women naturally wanted to stay at their quarters to look after the kids whilst the men went out to hunt.

However, there have been recent reports that, in actual fact, the women went out to hunt along with the men. This proves that it is not natural for a woman to want to just stay at home and let the man lead the way. However, I think that this panicked all the men in the Stone Age –

their plan to have their dinner made for them, and a sparkling abode to come home to after a hard day's work clubbing dinosaurs to death, wasn't quite going to plan. So I think that they made an SOS call to God for him to put more "Serve Men" chips in women and more "Asshole" ones in men. And so the suppressing of women's desires to have a life of their own and to just serve men was set in stone......well, at least that is what they had hoped.

I mean, think about it and it's pretty obvious that this "Serve Your Man" chip kicks in from a very early age: when girls are toddlers, we want to play "Mum", desperately craving for a life-like doll to hold in our arms, having to change its nappy and feed them when they cry. Then the housewife training kicks in: little domestic goddesses in the making, pretending to cook and clean in our own little play kitchen. I actually had a toy vacuum cleaner when I was little!!!

But it isn't only the "Serve Your Man" chip that has tried to keep women away from work and kept at home, there have been some cruel psychological tricks played as well.

In the past, in some major religions, women were branded "unclean" and "contaminators" if they had just given birth or were on their menstrual cycle!! Some societies even had a special hut that women were banished to whilst they were menstruating, so as not to come into contact with a male!

So it seems to me that this was God and his mates planning to keep women down and locked away so she wouldn't have a hope in hell of having any sort of career.

If Women Ruled The World...

Women deserve to be in a more authoritative role in the world, and we should be shouting just as loud as the men when it comes to flaunting our intelligence.

If women were more in charge, it would be a lot easier to juggle a career and motherhood, that's for sure.

Initially, after having a baby, women would really appreciate some flexibility from their employer, as it is emotionally tough going from spending every moment of the day with your baby for weeks/months, to then working five days a week and seeing them properly only at weekends.

'I'm Queen of the world!'

Women who have a high-flying career don't necessarily want to give up their job that they enjoy, but they seriously lose out because of inflexible employers not letting them work part-time or even just a few hours less a week, even though they would still be producing top quality work for the company.

So a lot of women end up having to take some time out of their career to be a good mother (and the fact that childcare is so damn expensive!) and then find it extremely difficult to return to the same job status a little later in life, enabling mostly men to steal all the good jobs!

According to the Equal Opportunities Commission, the number of women in highly paid jobs declines at the age of 30 and doesn't start to recover until 41. In contrast, the proportion of men in highly paid jobs continues to rise consistently up to age 46. And between the ages of 30 and 35, women without children are twice as likely to be in higher-paid jobs than mothers.

So it looks like women are still suffering for choosing to be a mother – equal opportunities my ass!

However, if it was mostly women in charge of businesses and large corporations, I believe it would be a different world. I'm sure that there would be plenty of flexibility so you could not only thrive on having a stimulating career, but also on having the time to be a great mother to your children.

There would also be much less aggression in the workplace - a lot more talking issues out, enabling a positive atmosphere, instead of flying off the handle to show power and create fear.

Take, for example, Oprah Winfrey – possibly the most successful woman in the history of television - she treats her staff to shopping sprees, encouraging a pleasant and constructive working environment. What a different approach to the usual hostile male one.

And there would be no need to power dress and act as "tough" as men to be taken seriously in the board room – your voice would actually be heard.

Planet earth would be a much more pleasurable place to be - there would be no wars. This is what God probably never quite anticipated when giving so much testosterone (assholeness) to men – too much fighting. I'm sure if we had had women world-leaders from the word go, the world would have a completely different history and a much more calmer present.

Honey, I'm Home!

Yes, women who only want to be a mother and wife are much rarer these days. Gone are the days of the "Stepford Wives" image - the male's idea of a picture perfect life with the immaculately dressed wife in her apron doing all her household chores, all the shopping, looking after the children and attending to her husbands needs

'Dinner's ready dear'

promptly, all with a gleaming smile and not a hair out of place.

Yes, the 1950's domestic goddess is long gone. Women really went all out - bras were burnt, equal pay fought for (well, we're still fighting for that one) – recognising that we, too, can have a career. I mean, this in itself is evidence that God gave men an easier time. Have men ever had to fight to be recognised in the work-place? Have men ever asked to have the same pay as women? And journeying back a bit, have men ever had to fight for the right to vote?

Bloody Hell......BML!

Yes, it's a tough world out there for a working lady, but being a Mum as well, just makes it even tougher. And even although women are wonderful at multi-tasking (another gene/chip in our DNA so that women always end up doing more chores than men), as mentioned before, I think God made it as difficult as possible for women to leave their child and still have a high flying career.

For instance, what about breastfeeding? How are women supposed to be in a high-flying job and still be able to perform this duty? I can hardly imagine a woman being in an important meeting, doing a power-point presentation, with a baby swinging from her breasts, having a hearty feed!

Ha! But we figured that one out God - we can express milk and leave it for the baby. So there!.......although, even though we figured that we could do that, we still have the embarrassing problem of BML - Breast Milk Leakage. It's just never ending for women!!

A lady I know of, who had just had a baby, was returning to work after her short maternity leave. She was sad at the fact that she had to express her milk (in which she felt like a dairy cow hooked up to the big pumps) in the morning for her Mother to feed her baby during the day, as she was aware of the physical and emotional bond between Mother and baby that breastfeeding provides.

However, what was upmost on her mind that day was her fight against BML. It is an understatement to say that she was quite overwhelmed in trying to decide what was the best solution for her to use in this battle - nursing pads, leakage inhibitors, nipple shields, breast shells, breast guards – she felt like she was a governments weapons inspector!

After finally deciding on the nursing pads, she was attending her first meeting in months, aching emotionally from being apart from her baby, but soaking up the atmosphere of being amongst adults and having her brain be alive again.......only that wasn't the only soaking up that she would be doing.

During the meeting, her "extra adhesive" pads fell away from her breasts down to her waist under her white blouse. Unaware of this, she started to feel her breast cramp up and braced herself for some leakage, fully expecting her pads to save the day, like Mighty Mouse powering into the sky with his fist in the air.

However, after people started talking to her breasts instead of her face, she glanced down and to her horror saw two huge wet patches with her nipples shining through her blouse like she was in a wet t-shirt competition.

'Erm, can I be excused please?'

She quickly folded her arms to disguise her soiled blouse, but after trying to make some notes with her arms attached to her breasts, which made her look like she was in a straight jacket, she finally made the decision to discontinue the freak show and excused herself from the meeting with a rather red face!

An Extra Portion Of Chips

Yes, being a Mother to an infant whilst trying to win the career woman of the year title is tricky. And it certainly doesn't get any easier as the infant grows.

Have you ever noticed that when children hurt themselves they always call for their Mother? Even when kids are ill at school, out comes the famous, 'I want my Mum,' phrase to the teacher, which consequently hauls you away from work. Now, as much as this, I'm sure, melts the hearts of all mothers everywhere, and your first instinct is to protect and comfort your child, don't you ever wonder why its never, 'I want my Dad?'

This is, I believe, because God has also planted little "Mum" chips inside children, so that they will always call out, 'Ma mere!' instead of, 'Mon pere!' A little far fetched you think? Think back to when you were a child, who did you always want to comfort you in times of need? I always called out for my Mum, even though my Dad spent lots of quality time with us as well.

I remember when I was only in primary two, which would make me just six years old. I was desperate for a pee whilst sitting in my tiny little chair as the teacher was talking at the front of the class. So I raised my little hand up and asked to go to the toilet, but was told frostily, 'YOU HAVE JUST COME BACK FROM BREAK-TIME, YOU SHOULD HAVE GONE THEN.' Crossing my legs, I couldn't hold on any longer and so relieved myself in my seat.

Now I was a strong and very determined little mite and so although I felt like crying when I realised that my seat was soaking wet and the floor below looked like it had experienced a torrential downpour, I held my emotions in and just took deep breaths, trying not to blurt out the "M" word.

Then, the boy who sat next to me nudged me on the shoulder and said that there was a little puddle of water next to my seat. Now, in not wanting to let on to anyone what had happened, I just said for him to, 'Mop it up then,' in a nonchalant manner. And that he did…using a paper towel! Ah bless! However, after a couple of minutes the teacher wondered what was going on and came to investigate.

In realising what had happened, she said that she would take me to get me cleaned up and offered me a spare pair of her underwear to wear….!! Two things now concern me, 1: Did she actually think that a grown woman's pants would actually fit around my teeny-weeny bottom? And 2: More to the point, why did she have a spare pair of pants with her? Mm.

Anyway, after politely refusing her pants and then the embarrassment of walking out of the class with a saturated behind in front of all my classmates, it all became too much, and the most popular slogan from children all over the world shot out from my mouth, 'I WANT MY MUM!' This came out without even thinking, it was instinct, or, as I would put it, the "chip" at work. I mean, why didn't I blurt out 'Dad?'

Human Metal Detector

And there is even more expected of a mother - they are the ones who are expected to know where everything is, which steals even more time away from doing something just for you.

'MUM, WHERE'S MY SOCK?' 'MUM, WHERE'S MY FOOTBALL BOOT?' And the amazing thing is, is that mums always do know where they are (how is that???). My Dad was always famous for, 'You better ask your Mum,' as he didn't really do many household chores when I was little, and my Mum had a full-on "Serve Your Man" chip in her.

Yes, it seems that a woman's work is certainly never done and all because of God's almighty plan. Yes, the "chips" we have been given are strong! We must be aware of when they are activated and not succumb to their powers!

Chapter Eight

Tick-Tock

Now, if you are in your late twenties/early thirties and haven't yet taken the plunge into motherhood as you have been holding off until you have achieved your career goals, or you may simply have not yet met the man of your dreams, this is when you may become aware of a little ticking sound.

Time Is Running Out!

Yes, it's the old familiar sound of the biological clock that ticks away every day with a deafening tick-tock, to let women know that there is an alarm due to go off at some stage in the near future, telling us that our time is up. Faced with an image comparable to an hourglass egg timer with the sand rapidly dropping to the bottom, we are under immense pressure to utilize our eggs before the use-by-date - or they will simply "go off".

'I'm really not impressed at the rate that sand is dropping to the bottom!'

Yes, at this stage in life, we have to start thinking strategically. It's no longer about "playing the field" and, 'I'll just wait and see where this relationship goes.' No, it's now about, 'Is he the one?' 'Would he make a good father?' and if not then, 'Get the hell out of here, I'm on a mission!'

Apparently, grown women are supposed to conceive easiest in their early twenties. However, most young women at this age are either mostly career focused or still just trying to figure out what the hell they want to do with their lives. Becoming a Mother is usually the last thing on their mind. Most women in their early to mid twenties would rather travel the world and *experience* life before actually *creating* it. Plus, a lot of women this age haven't even met their ideal partner yet!

I recently read that if you want to make sure that you have a healthy child, you should conceive by the age of 30, and that a women's fertility peaks at the ripe old age of 24. The article went on to say that 32 is still ok, but not ideal, but by the age of 35, your chances of conception start to go down hill and your child could have some anomalies. Plus, you have an increased chance of breast cancer if you have your first baby over the age of 30.

Ok, I have to say that I am highly concerned. No, I am panicked!! This is so ridiculous and out of order from God! Give women a chance!

Note to God: We no longer live in biblical times and get married at the age of around 14 and so by the age of 18 are more than ready to start a family. Eh, hello God? Get with the times. This is the 21st century! Women should be able to have children for as long as men can! A great big "up you" from God to women there, I think.

I mean, here women are, almost incapable of having children after our mid-late thirties, with men being able to go forth and multiply for donkeys years - even when they are old, grey, wrinkly, and great, great, great grandfathers. It so unfair! For women, if you haven't had a baby by mid-30's, then tough – you're either never going to or are probably going to need the assistance of IVF.

Sisters Doing It For Themselves!

So with your biological clock stridently and expeditiously ticking by, you think that you better take the plunge and have a baby whilst you've still got the chance. But what if you haven't yet met the man of your dreams?

Thousands of women at this age haven't but they can't exactly wait around for Prince Charming to show up - we don't have the luxury of time like the males. So thousands of women are taking action themselves and are resorting to ordering batches of sperm to go, before their eggs do a disappearing act. So at least, I suppose, in this way, women can pick and choose candidates with some good healthy genes on 'em - but at a cost. Women have spent untold thousands on hormone treatments in a constant bid to get pregnant. And women are emotionally well spent too – disappointment with unsuccessful inseminations and suffering miscarriages all takes its toll.

Yes, whilst women are going through an emotional and financial rollercoaster ride, guys of a similar age still don't have a care in the world and are usually having a grand, trouble-free time spending their money on fast cars and typical boys toys.

Another expensive method women are resorting to in order to have a little rug rat, is freezing their eggs. This takes so much pressure off of a woman. Prolonging her chance of having kids enables her to focus solely on her career for longer and is also a safety net in case all her eggs have deserted her when she finally meets her knight in shining armour.

However, although not having to listen to your biological clock quite as much is a magnificent thing, it does have its downsides…surprise, surprise. It is, again, financially costly, with also a possible increased risk of having a congenitally abnormal baby and, in the end, you still have no guarantee of becoming pregnant!

Double Standards - Again!!

Yes, trying to defy the biological cut off point to have a baby is tough, but one "mature" lady succeeded. The oldest woman to date to give birth was 67 - but that was with *donated* eggs and IVF. So it wasn't really the woman's biological child, hence it wasn't a true defiance of God's "arrangement".

Now, perhaps a lot would argue that this is too old anyway and how can a woman of such an age have the energy and time on her hands to give a child a wonderful upbringing? However, what concerns me the most is why men and women are treated differently on this subject.

Nobody bats an eyelid when men become fathers in *their* 50's and 60's. Look at Michael Douglas. He became a father again most recently at the age of 59. Paul McCartney became a father again at 61. The amusing thing was, that whilst I was trying to find information on what age Sir Paul was when he fathered a child with Heather Mills, all of the data that appeared on my Google search was, *'Paul is delighted,' 'We are delighted.'* Such a complete contrast to my findings when researching the woman that had twins at 67: *'Elderly woman gives birth,' 'This is wrong,'* and, *'It's a scandal!'*

I think that there's one rule for the female sex here and another for the male. The list goes on for older men fathering children: Rod Stewart was 60 when his fiancé Penny Lancaster became pregnant. The world's oldest father Nanu Ram Jogi had another child at the age of 90! And the start of the article was almost triumphant: *'The world's oldest father has done it again!'*

Time For A Change

So it seems that once a woman reaches the grand old age of 35, that's when it all starts to go down hill, and before you know it, you are staring the menopausal years straight in the eye.

Yes, those brief childbearing years have passed quicker than Lewis Hamilton doing a lap in a Grand Prix, and after a few pre-menopausal years, where you had hoped that your irregular periods were just due to being stressed, it's all of a sudden on you – yes, its THE CHANGE.

Yes, its time to crank up all the symptoms and experience them all at once: the hot flushes, decreased libido, thinning of hair, mood swings, the sense of doom, insomnia, fatigue, bladder problems, vaginal problems, and memory loss (my Mother often goes into a room and can't remember what she is there for - and my favourite one is where she is looking for her glasses that are already in her hands!).

Oh, and I almost forgot to mention that women's collagen levels lessen considerably with menopause, causing dry, flaky "alligator" type skin and wrinkles. Mm, my, I am so looking forward to this stage.

That's It - Period

I mean, women can't catch a break. For years women's lives have been dictated to by their periods. Holidays have been scheduled around menstrual due dates, sex put on hold, and having to spend our hard earned cash on sanitary wear every month (it's so unfair that women have to part with some of their money every month to buy tampons and pads, when we could be buying a nice bottle of wine for the same money instead. And what makes it even more annoying, is that men can invest their wage wholly on things that only bring them joy).

And so just when we think we are free from this dictatorship, we are then laden with all the unbelievably depressing symptoms of the menopause. So the struggle continues for women.

But just when you think that the whole menstrual cycle palaver is over completely – it can come back with a vengeance. I know of one menopausal woman who was sitting in a meeting at work and had an unexpected visit. She was utterly shocked as she thought that her periods were over, kaput. It was so embarrassing for her, with blood on her seat and not knowing whether to just sit there or to get up.

I mean, what a cruel and unfair design from God – letting women think that their menstruating era was over, when it really isn't. And men never have such worries as in, 'Mm, I hope a pool of blood doesn't come rushing out of me today.'

Yes, the "change" can be quite unpredictable at times. I suppose it is similar to going through puberty - transforming from one person to another - and it can be a scary and quite an overwhelming time for a woman.

My Mum is currently suffering from an increased bout of nerves, along with a feeling of dread, and so is a little bit of a nightmare to be with in a car at the moment. *Every time* when I am driving, she continually points out that there is a car in front of me, with which I "kindly" reply that I am quite aware of and that it is not that uncommon - considering that I am driving on a public road! Then she starts to use the invisible break on her side - slamming her foot down onto NOTHING in the passenger seat, as if that is going to stop the car. I have to add that this is a little infuriating and has caused a few, ahem, "debates".

To Dye For!

Yes, this time of a woman's life can be trying, in particular on the sweating side of things.

My friend's Mum takes a little hand-sized battery powered fan with her almost everywhere she goes. Yes, it has become a regular occurrence to have a little trickle of sweat run down her chest accompanied with a rosy-cheeked face due to the hot flushes. I suppose, however, this does have its

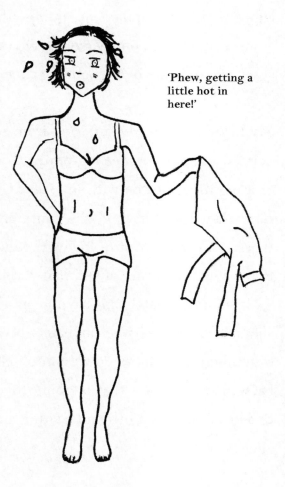

'Phew, getting a little hot in here!'

benefits; she never has to put too much blusher on, saving her money in the long run when buying cosmetics.

Ok, that was a long shot. But I thought I would try and find some contradictory evidence that God surely can't be this cruel to the female species??? Ok, you're right, God is that cruel, and in particular to one poor lady at a party.

A woman I know of was at a Tupperware party and started having a hot flush whilst the hostess was talking to her about all the different types of tubs. Sweating profusely, she couldn't sit and listen anymore, so excused herself to go to the bathroom, so she could splash her face with some cold water. But as she got up from the cream leather sofa, and turned to get her bag, she and the hostess discovered a big blue patch where she had been sitting - the dye had run from her denim skirt due to her producing so much heat! I think the hostess has now invested in some throws for her sofa!

Hair We Go Again!

Another matter concerning dye is the one we use on our hair. Yes, at the menopausal stage, you no longer have just a few strands of hair that are grey. If the truth be told, you probably have a head full of the little blighters.

Now the same could be said for men at the same age, but God has made it easier for them – again.

Yes, it is highly annoying and obvious that God purposely tampered with our eyesight so that everyone thinks men look good with grey/white hair - it is actually quite sexy, damn it! They can get away with it! But when women decide to let their hair go "au natural" and the little grey wiry buggers start to come out, there are only a few, select, women who can look good on it. Grey hair generally ages women by about 10 years, and they look less attractive - and this isn't just applicable to menopausal women!

When thirty-something Jennifer Lopez turned up at an awards ceremony with grey roots, the pictures of her in the next day's tabloids zoomed in on them, proclaiming this '*Shocking*!' and, '*She will be getting scripts sent to her to play all the Mother roles.*' Yet all George Clooney gets with his salt and pepper locks is, '*He looks so sexy.*' This is unfair again! So basically, men don't have to bother to cover their greys and they still look great, but women have to go and spend a fortune in the hair salon every couple of months so that we won't look like our great-grandmother!

So Crossed Over The Line!

Yes, fighting the signs of aging is tough for a grown woman of any age. However, it's particularly difficult when going through the menopause, what with our collagen levels becoming more and more depleted, and how we are so forgetful we can't for the life of us remember what the name of that eye cream was we saw advertised. But what probably makes it even more of a difficult time to swallow, is that even though men also get lines and folds, they – yes – again – have a much easier time of it.

Yes, it so annoying that men with wrinkles and scars are deemed "sexy" and "ruggedly handsome" and women with creases and crinkles are labelled as "past it", "unattractive" and told, 'Quick, get a chemical peel!'

Yes, I think this is another consequence of God tampering with our eyesight, so that it yet again gives the guys an undemanding life. So men can yet again save their money, as they don't have to run out and buy the latest super-duper wrinkle-free cream, spend all their pennies on expensive salon treatments, and have their face paralysed with Botox!

Yes, it's a long hard struggle being the female of the species. But surely, *surely*, after all this menopause malarkey, this must be the end of all the embarrassing and invasive events in a lady's life? Don't be silly – it continues.

Chapter Nine

Just When You Thought The Coast Was Clear

As if women haven't been through enough already, what with their periods, invasive examinations, giving birth, the menopause, alligator skin...oh no, its not over yet...here comes the time for a Pelvic Organ Prolapse! Yahoo!

I mean, c'mon God, give us a break here. Haven't we endured enough pain in our lifetime???

Approximately one out of three women aged 45 or older has some degree of prolapse. And by age 80, more than one out of every 10 women will have undergone surgery for a prolapse!! And a lot of the time it is because women's muscles have become weaker after giving birth. It's just never ending!

Yes, just as you were thinking the coast was clear, your pelvic organs begin to fail you, and your Urethra, Uterus, Vagina, Small Bowel and Rectum (oh, is that all?!) can all start to head south. And the names of the surgeries to treat them are quite daunting also: Vaginal Vault Prolapse Surgery, Cystocele Surgery, with the most horrifying one being, Vaginal OBLITERATION!!!!!!! The surgeries sounds more like doing a round in Gymnastics and then going into battle at war!

Circle Of Truth

One (*very*) elderly female I know has had a few pelvic problems of late and I'm not quite sure what procedure she has done, but it does not sound good. Yes, unfortunately, due to her age, she is deemed too old to go under anaesthetic, so she has to have a little rubber style ring placed inside her every six months. Now this may not seem too unpleasant on the ear but believe me, it's not pretty. Just as I was biting into a Jammie Dodger, I was given the gory details of how her "ring" regularly gets, well, "entangled", and how it can be a real fight to get it out, and, well, I think I need say no more.

So perhaps women should have the surgery to repair their pelvic problems whilst they can - as annoying as that is!

It's Getting Invasive - Again

Another surgery to deal with pelvic prolapses, and not mentioned so far, is the much looked forward to HYSTERECTOMY! Yes, if there is no other option to sort your sagging uterus out or if you have some other painful situation going on that no other op will fix, then you are left with the mother of all operations.

Yes, ladies, it's time to have the second most "popular" operation after the C-section. Yep, it's yet another embarrassing and invasive procedure to have done, and with some new choices to make along with it too: will it be a Total Hysterectomy, a Subtotal/Partial Hysterectomy or should you opt for the totally Radical one? (I take it, that in this instance, they're not using the slang definition for the word radical, meaning "awe-inspiring?" Ok, I know that was wishful thinking)

Yes girls, like me, if you are still what is classed as a "young" woman in her twenties or thirties, you still have all this to look forward to. And to all the women who are either at this stage or have passed it: well done, you deserve a medal.

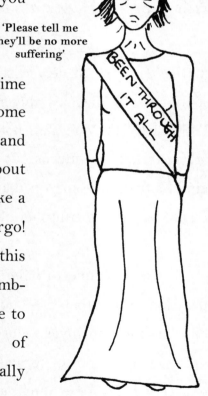

'Please tell me they'll be no more suffering'

I mean, this should be a time in a woman's life to have some spare time on her hands and be able to feel good about herself - not having to make a list of surgeries to undergo! And on top of all this unreasonable bodily bombardment, we then also have to deal with the issue of beginning to feel sexually invisible to society.

A Shadow Of Your Former Self

Yes, it seems all too long ago when you were once hounded, harassed and wolf-whistled at as you strutted your stuff past the extremely "friendly" builders on the scaffolding site. Now, however, instead of the builders asking for your number, they're asking if you need help crossing the street – well, not quite, but not far away! And you can hear a pin drop in this new deafening silence, with the only whistle coming from the wind, which is hurtling the tumbleweed by.

Yes, as much as you once complained and "tutted" at all the unwanted attention you used to get, suddenly you perhaps find yourself missing it in a way (I know, it's a horrible thing to admit!)

So women, at this stage in life, have to kind of accept being labelled as, 'Aw, what a sweet lady,' as opposed to, 'Phwoar, she's hot!' But in a bid not to feel too depressed, we just accept we now have wrinkles and that gravity is doing its job, and so shift our attention from the ridiculously impossible task of trying to appear like an

airbrushed model to the more enjoyable things in life –
perhaps studying wine, learning a different language and,
to hell with it, more holidays stuffing our face! Who cares
if we put a couple of pounds on? (Certainly not the
builders that's for sure)

Double Whammy!

Yes, having the hysterectomy and then feeling like a
ghost to the opposite sex is just adding insult to injury. I
mean, trying to combat wrinkles and droopy boobs along
with having to face the possibility of having your ovaries
taken away and your vagina shrunk (!!), is just a step too
far! I mean, way to go God to make us feel even less like a
real woman!

And you can forget about that holiday to the Med 'cos
you'll hardly be able to even move for 2 months after the
big op! There goes your sex life down the drain too – and
possibly the worst of the lot - you have to rely on your
man to cook for you!

Kitchen Nightmares!

Now, granted, a lot of men nowadays actually do do a bit of the cooking, but men of my, ahem, Father's generation, well, can't quite get the hang of it.

My Mum had a hysterectomy when I was only about 13. However, instead of worrying about the major surgery her body was about to endure, her major concern was for her family and how we would cope without her for 4 whole days. She was very apprehensive about leaving my Dad, my 2 brothers and myself to fend for ourselves whilst she was going to be in hospital, but we survived…just.

I did some housework and even cooked (well, my Mum had left things in the freezer for me to heat in the oven, but still, I thought I did rather well compared to my brothers who did absolutely squat…but now that I think about it, that was probably my "Serve Men" chip at work).

I think that she was perhaps most worried about my Dad, as he had had quite a few mishaps in the kitchen before - and the fact that beans on toast was his speciality.

Once he tried to boil an egg.......in the microwave! This was when I was about 11, and I was in my room reading, when I all of a sudden heard this almighty BANG! I ran downstairs and saw that the kitchen was covered in egg yolk with my Dad standing still, speechless, in the middle of the floor. I remember howling with laughter, especially when I noticed that there was a lump of egg on the top of his head. And that was only my Mum leaving him for just half an hour to run an errand!

So considering that a woman who has just undergone a hysterectomy isn't even supposed to make herself a cup of tea — the kettle is deemed too heavy to lift - it is an understatement to say that my mother was a little apprehensive to see what assortment of ingredients was to greet her on her return from the hospital.

I think it's fair to say that unless your man is Gordon Ramsay or Jamie Oliver, having your other half do the cooking for you after your op can be quite a scary ride!

A Bit Of Hollywood Glamour!

Yes, recovering from a hysterectomy can be very challenging, not only to one's palette, but to your energetic lifestyle too. My friend's mother, who is always full of zip, practically had to be tied down to the sofa so she couldn't reach for the vacuum or be able to grab hold of a cloth and start to polish after her hysterectomy (why she just didn't enjoy not having to do the housework was beyond me and my friend, but maybe it was her "Serve Your Man" chip that was making her think crazy thoughts of, 'The woman must do everything').

However, what concerned my friend most about her Mother's behaviour after the operation was that she was scratching "downstairs" a lot. So one afternoon, she bit the bullet and asked what was her problem - just why was she so damn itchy?

To her horror, she discovered that she had been shaved - completely! My friend was quite distressed. Her mother had been shaved so the surgeon could see better! Now this may be common knowledge to a lot of people, but to my friend (and to me!), it was quite shocking. I mean, you go in for an op, and you come out with a complimentary Hollywood!

I've asked my friend that if I ever have to have an op "down there", then to please remind me that they do this, so I can book an appointment with a qualified beautician so I can get a proper Hollywood and not a shoddy one done with a razor!

Don't Make Me Laugh!

So, you're recovering from the hysterectomy, coming to terms with being sexually undesirable to the general public, and so you are pretty much thinking that this must be your lot, that there can surely be no other misfortune heading your way. Only one day, when someone tells a hilarious joke, you laugh as normal, but this time, you realise that a little bit of wee came out also!!! Yes, time for a little bit of URINARY INCONTINENCE! Whilst you've experienced a little of this during your pregnancy years, it seems that its catching up with you - again.

Yes, it seems there is no escape and certainly no end to a woman's suffering. After the menopause there can be an oestrogen deficiency, which can cause the bladder control muscles to become weak. And after a hysterectomy, the urinary tract can be damaged. So women are now scared to laugh, cough, or even sneeze in case it leads to an emergency change of underwear.

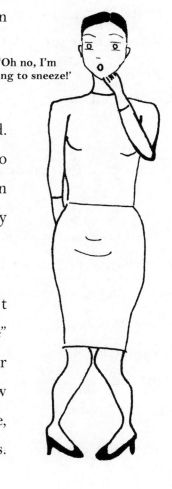

'Oh no, I'm going to sneeze!'

And, after thinking that you don't have to buy any "feminine care" products anymore now that your periods are over, you are now back in that aisle, only this time, going after the incontinence pads.

Now, yes, men do suffer from incontinence too - but it's twice as common in women as it is in men - surprise, surprise!

I was recently in a public toilet and noticed a poster on the cubicle door with a really worried looking woman on it with the slogan, 'I'M DREAMING OF A DRY CHRISTMAS.' In the cubicle next to me, I heard the voice of a little girl ask her Mum, 'Why does that woman look so sad?' Poor little mite - little does she know what the future holds.

Fancy A Squeeze?

And there's more. Yes, it's not just a woman's nether regions that are invaded again at this stage of a woman's life. I mean, you would think that having to have the Hysterectomy op or the Vaginal Obliteration was enough invasion for a good while and hopefully the last one of your life. But don't be silly - God obviously needs some more amusement.

This is when women also get the call for a mammogram! Yes, another painful examination. Now, granted, they do save lives and the medical staff, are, I'm sure, full of the best intentions, but I'm sure there must be another way of detecting any abnormalities instead of having your breasts squeezed to a pulp as if trying to extract juice from them.

Could you imagine them doing this to guys to check for testicular cancer? 'Yes sir, if you could just place your testicles in this device so that we can squeeze, pull and pound them 'til they're blue to see if there are any lumps.' You wouldn't see them for dust!

So, I think its high time that God realised that what women go through is maybe fun for him and his "soul mates", but it certainly isn't for women. He needs to start to change his ways a little and give women a break. I received an email recently that summed women's experiences up:

MENstrual Cramps, MENopause, GUYnecologist and when we have REAL problems its a HISterectomy. Ever noticed how all of women's problems start with MEN?

Yes, it's time for a change all right. A few of my suggestions/orders are to follow.

Chapter Ten

Time For An Upgrade

I'm sure that by now, after reading all of my evidence in this book, you agree with me that God is definitely a male - one of the guys - who definitely gave men an easier time of it.

Batting For The Other Team

Whilst writing this book, I have obviously made my feelings clear to my partner, David. However there was one night, after a bottle of wine or three, when we were deep in discussion/debate about this subject, that I - and I say this lightly - started to feel slightly less hard done by and saw things from more of a male perspective.

I mean, David argued that guys suffer too and that God may well be a woman because God gave guys a pair of testicles, 'AND THEY CAN HURT!' he proclaimed. 'Ok, I can take that point,' I said.

Then David got on a roll: 'And it may be women who suffer the rollercoaster ride of emotions every month due to PMT, but it's us guys that have to put up with you when you are like Jekyll and Hyde!' 'Ok, point number two taken – just,' was my slurred response. An animated David then went on to describe how he had heard of a woman that head-butted her boyfriend when it was a certain time of the month.

It was this persuasive and somewhat intoxicated argument that made me have a momentary lapse of insanity and made me look at being a woman as more of a blessing than a curse.

'I mean, ok, maybe having to carry the baby in pregnancy is a wonderful thing,' I garbled, 'I've heard some women actually miss being pregnant; they miss feeling their child growing inside of them and the wonder of creating life and men can feel jealous of this experience. And maybe women have it easier when it comes to dating – it is, after all, usually men that have to make the first move to initiate any potential romance. And maybe it's better to have lots of choice of what to wear and buy compared with men. Sure it takes longer to get ready, but we do always seem to steal the show when entering a party and its always so much more interesting to watch the women arrive at the Oscars instead of the men.'

Reality Check

'What am I doing? Brrr. Ok, shake it off! There is no way I am being converted! That is enough of that!' I proclaimed, coming to my senses with David then hanging his head in commiseration. That wine was strong!

Ok, I can perhaps retract a *couple* of my powerful feelings about God being a hasty designer after hearing my boyfriend's argument - but not too much. I mean there are just certain things that I definitely cannot and will not ever get on board with, and nobody will ever convince me otherwise: Body Hair Removal, Periods, Cellulite, BML, Labour, Invasive Vaginal Examinations,

The Menopause, and The Hysterectomy. That's a hell of a lot of stuff to deal with! Men just can't compete – EVER!!

So I think it's high time the female anatomy was re-addressed. I mean, I understand that God perhaps had other things on his mind at the time of designing humanity - deciding on who was destined to meet who, and where and when, and then trying to balance the world out with a certain degree of free will - and so maybe it wasn't just his wicked sense of humour (I am definitely not meaning the slang sense of the word "wicked", meaning "very impressive") that was the reason he unloaded all of the ridiculous and painful stuff onto the females. Maybe it was to also help immediately reduce his over-whelming workload.

But I don't think that there is room for too many excuses, and lets face it, he still favoured the guys. So, I think that in the 21st century, God could really do with updating his collection a little – OK – A LOT! I mean, yes, I get that he perhaps has quite a lot to contend with even now, what with all the prayers that he answers around the world for famine, war, crime and, in general, saving peoples lives.

Sit Up And Pay Attention – This Is Serious!

But I think that you should definitely take on board what I am saying, God. Yes, I'm talking directly to you now, as I feel there can be no more messing about. You need to, firstly, before sorting out some of the problems of womankind that I am going to suggest, admit that you stuck up for your own gender and didn't consider (care) what females would have to go through - as we would like an apology please.

Now, you'd better be listening to me, as I know that you made men to only use a small part of their brain when people are talking to them compared to women, who use a large part of their brain, so that men can just switch off when we are telling them something meaningful (which is just infuriating!).

So, ears open and your full brain switched on please - here are a few of my simple tips that millions of women around the globe would be extremely grateful for if you upgraded to:

- **No Body Hair** – this would be extremely wonderful and very well received as it would be a massive time saver and also a lot less pain in our lives

- **No Periods** – I mean, obviously we still want to have children, but if you could find a way of no more painful and inconvenient monthly bleeding to enable us to do so, then that would be greatly appreciated

- **Pregnancy** – Please can you find a way to allow us to still drink alcohol when with child, so it won't affect the baby - this would help us get through the 9 months in good spirits

- **Labour** – Now if you could implant a little switch in women so that we could easily turn off the pain whilst going through this experience, that would be just dandy

- **Menopause** – I think a little more time to conceive a child would be great, so I think you should increase our egg volume substantially. And, when we do finally reach the menopause, I would really find a way to stop all the hot flushes and sweats, cos' that's just not a good look for a woman

- **Cellulite** – Yes, I think a little less fat cells in the thigh and hip area would make for more of an attractive package – so then we wouldn't have to work out as much and spend all our money on creams that don't work

'But I thought you were all going to visualise your genes/chips to have a lesser impact on your body, why do you need **me** to fix everything?' I hear you say, God. Well, yes, even though women are wonderful at multi-tasking (yes, we know it's your doing God, so guys end up doing less), us women trying to lessen the impact of our "chips" to achieve those results may just take up too much of our time – we can't do *everything*!

So, God, I believe it's your call – and plus, I think you need to realise that this might actually be a good thing for you!

Yes, I think that if you take just those little tips on board, then you are going to have a much happier world on your hands. I mean, think about it: less prayers and anger pointed at you from women to stop their pain, which means you will have more free time on your hands to do whatever you want. I mean, I don't know whatever it is that you do in your spare time, but why not just have a chill-out for a day here and there? It's always important to make time for yourself, you know.

And think about women not having periods every month: NO PMT! This would not only be amazing for women, but men wouldn't have to put up with anymore "Jekyll & Hyde" outbursts too, resulting in much less aggravation for the guys. And you've always had all your mates best interests at heart, haven't you?

On My Knees Here!

I mean, ok, perhaps us women (and men) on earth right now will not benefit from those upgrades, but I feel it my duty to fight for a better world for the future generations of women to come - just as we are fighting global warming for our children's, children's children.

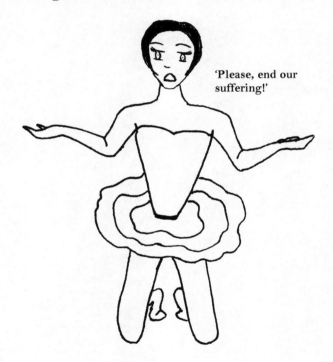

'Please, end our suffering!'

So, I implore you to make the necessary changes I have suggested. Remove those ridiculous genes/chips you have given us and replace them with more rational and well thought-out ones, before another load of poor souls (quite literally) come to earth to be women......and also, come to think of it, if there is such a thing as re-incarnation, I sure as hell don't want to go through all this shit again!

www.godmustbeaman.com

www.elizabethcaproni.com